P9-BHW-831

SCANDINAVIAN

BY

PAUL TWITCHELL

Letters to Gail
Volume II

Printed in U.S.A.

ISBN: 0-88155-024-8

Fourth Printing 1986

ECKANKAR
P.O. Box 27300
Minneapolis, MN 55427 U.S.A.

Preface

Letters to Gail, Volume II, is the conclusion to the 100 letters that Paul Twitchell wrote from December 6, 1962, until July 14, 1963, to Gail, his future wife.

ECKANKAR is pleased to present to you the complete set of letters, for it was Gail's wish that the teachings in these letters be shared with others.

It is a rare thing to find that the principles and yardsticks for measuring life can be given with the kindness and genuine sense of freedom that is found within these pages.

The Editors

TABLE OF CONTENTS

Letters to Gail

May 5, 1963

Dear Gail:

Values is the subject of this letter. A value which we are interested in is that which serves as a quality for the individual's inner life. Naturally the outer value of life can be based upon money or those qualities known to society as honesty, fair treatment, altruism, respectability, esteem, love, kindness, etc. Naturally there can be negative or positive qualities upon which one bases his life. These are interwoven with the attitudes of life, right and wrong as the religion of the individual or the society in which he lives determines.

One wouldn't expect the natives of North Borneo to behave or have the same values as the European and American civilizations. Neither do you expect the Communistic values to be the same as our values are. In this lies the answer to many questions as we read occurring daily throughout the world. This is why each dictator wants his nation or subjects to accept his standard of values for this means that he will have them thinking in his world of regulations and rules. Therefore he will be the master over them.

To have control or leadership over anyone or any group one must get his subjects to accept his standard of values. This is in any field of endeavor—for example, any religion which wants a large congregation must establish a set of values for its people. Take the case of the Christian Cross: to the Christian it is everything and holds his highest esteem in values which consist of suffering, and the commandments of God as laid down in the Bible concerning: Honoring the parents, murder, adultery, stealing, false witness, etc. But to a Zen Buddhist these would be children's sop, for they have a higher value to look forward to, and put into their conscience as a part of themselves. To an old Roman his highest value was his armour hung on a tree stump in his garden. From that point all his moral and ethical world revolved.

The average man is concerned with life, liberty and the pursuit of happiness; but the saint is concerned with death of self, obedience to divine will (intuition), divine love, and the virtues of humility, patience, purity, fidelity, faith and service. His life was one of prayer, penitence, repentance. These ideas are common to those interested in the religious life. Now the social order of this day lays down another set of values for you to follow: personal honor, national honor, friendship, loyalty, reverence of the dead, free enterprise, personal initiative, etc., including teamwork.

When you put these together in a comparison the question is: Just where does this fit in your own world? This is a question that every individual must answer for himself, for if he doesn't fit himself into the rigid mentality of the society's values he is considered an oddball. If he lives his life according to the religious values set down by the order of church in which he belongs, like the Mennonites, then he is completely out of this civilization. Nobody wants to mingle with him because he is out of order, so they think, because his outlook on life is different, his values are different. For example, the Mennonite doesn't believe in automobiles. He puts his values in the horse and buggy, dark clothes, self-education, restrictions of marriage within one group, nonresistance, plainness of dress, restriction of environment to own group, and money only for the purchase of those goods they cannot raise or make. So you see a group of this nature has nothing to do with what we call civilization's values.

I am spending a letter on this subject so you can get acquainted with moral theology, group ethics, and historical values, all intermingling with one another. Sociology, which is a study of the origin and evolution of society, or of the forms, institutions and functions of human groups, is actually a study of the values of mankind which we have in our present society; that as an industrial civilization we are controlled by the merchants and manufacturers, and since the manufacturers must overproduce in order to keep people working, therefore the masses must be whipped up to overconsumption. This is where advertising makes its stand to keep the individual's desire for material things whetted. So what happens? The emphasis is changed for the individual's outlook on what is the value to himself—he thinks that by wearing a Brooks Bros. suit he is placed in the position of top-man and that this is great. It means simply this: The values of life are placed upon vanity—have a fine auto, good home, fine wife and children, be a good citizen, have good clothes, and a houseful of gadgets, washing machines, dish-washers, TV, etc. This makes the wage-earner spend all his salary, get into debt, put his wife to work, and put the children to work during their spare hours. What I'm saying is the materialists through propaganda make the average man put his values outside himself. He has no value judgment. He is willing to cheat or rob if he could get away with it, not because it would be against his moral conscience. Most men are thieves at heart, but the fear of social stigma or imprisonment or fear of the law will keep them within the boundary.

Group values, like I've pointed out, are generally legalized like the Civil Rights Law, Fair Trade Law, Discrimination in Housing, etc. Individual values are set by recognized qualities in the individual—honesty, loyalty, unselfishness, etc.—and regulated by social recognition or ostracism, and through civil law. The teaching of this comes through education in schools, religions, and home. He who grows up to become a rebel against society and doesn't obey individual values as laid down by a society suffers through civil law, or ostracism; this includes sex life, social life, economic life, etc. The basis of this principle underlying man-made values is that man must work to earn his keep, he must obey the rules of society and he must respect the values given him.

Why am I discussing this matter? Simply for this reason. Life is actually not based upon these man-made values or virtues. They are for those in control for the subjugation of the masses, earning profits and keeping a grip upon controlling the minds and appetites of peoples. An old saying goes like this: "All laws are made by those for their own benefit!" Remember what I said about the writers of the Constitution: It was for their own benefit to control the mobs and save their own property. So it is your duty to become higher than man-made values! Look down at them, but serve God only, through what are His values. These are: divine love, being true to your ideal, unattachment, discrimination, forgiveness, etc. One gets these through insight, opening his consciousness to the Absolute, and getting himself divine wisdom. It is only through divine wisdom that one learns all the values of life—the real ones—and knows how to apply them.

Once you learn what the values of life are, and how to apply them through discrimination and unattachment, nothing else can ever touch you, and your life will make that step upon the path, lifting you above the actual struggles of mankind. You will learn to see everything with tolerance, humor and divine goodwill. It is amazing what will begin to happen to your whole life.

More later.

Letters to Gail

May 6, 1963

Dear Gail:

On the subject of time—space and time are not the framework of nature but of the world of the sense perception. Time cannot exist without an observer, and what you see as objective time really doesn't exist.

Man's perception of time is indicated by the clock. If he has a habit of working by the clock, newspaper, etc., life becomes fast. Events which are the agents of time move rapidly. Physical events and characteristics come into existence when an observer is present to witness with sound, touch, sight, smell, etc. Time is not real, for if it was it must involve change, and since there are no events except in present when the observer is there, and this is always the present. Remember what Blake said in one of his poems about the Halls of Los, where all events were frozen until you turned your attention upon them. So you see history is only a recorded document of those events which individuals saw in their own present-time. You see Time is dependent upon the individual's sense organs.

Actually time and space cannot be separated. Space in itself and time in itself sink into mere shadows and only a kind of union of the two preserves an existence; and this again depends on the observer's system of reference. Henri Bergson takes up the study of time in his book The Creative Mind, *and one point he makes is that even outside of physical time, where there is what might be called eternity, are rest points; that we can go so far and must come to rest points – in other words even the Soul moves from rest point to rest point. An interesting thought, isn't it?*

The past and future overlap and mingle. We look at the years which suddenly disappear because we are living in the present and suddenly that which we call time on which we base our whole existence itself no longer exists. It does not alter its position any more than space because it begins in the center of every event and every event is fixed in the center, and all that goes past from end to end of our life without moving by a hair's breath around its motionless pivot. Therefore time as an objective reality is false, and is only a relative.

The particular time-structure of your world-image is but your way of interpreting the ever-present reality. It is, with its structure of past, present and future, the product of your externalized world-image. Since time is an illusion then science cannot solve a problem born of it; each person has his individual time of perception and it is no other than his own unique experience. The movement of time is largely within each individual, and therefore is an abstract. But when an abstraction is taken to be something itself real it contradicts itself.

We must learn to conquer illusion (maya is the Indian word for illusion) before we can know reality. In the world of the Real, or God, we can only transcend the illusion of being a physical thing, and know ourselves as the spiritual entity. Therefore we are seeking an insight into the illusion known as time and find eternity. This world is limited to a three dimensional world: time, space and matter. If we can rise above these three parts of the physical world, there will be a transcendence of the consciousness to a higher level and we can have a wider perspective and a greater awareness.

In the physical life we clutch at the hours and days of the past and present to reassure ourselves, to fasten on some certainty, to convince ourselves that we are still in our right place in this life where all is substantial and real. Time is actually on one plane but man can live in several planes, according to his own psychic development. Therefore, man doesn't have to be bound by time, nor held back by the weight of his flesh; he can be anywhere he desires in his other self, as pointed out several times to you. If you will notice the mind measures the flight of time, and to some degree also measures it. Relativity teaches us that form which time takes in experience it never final, and vice versa, meaning that no experience is ever final as long as it's in time, and Karma; not until one is lifted into the higher planes, those above time. None in flesh will experience this until he has freed himself from the purely human angle of vision, and until this is done truth and God is hidden from him. To study this we must think: "What is my relation with time?" So when you think about any event, you place yourself mentally at a certain place and in a certain time, but it is not a true place nor a true time. To enter into the true place and true time one must follow out the dictates of the Shariyat-Ki-Sugmad which says that you must surrender the mind in order to see God.

Letters to Gail

Einstein's theory of relativity says that all time is local. Therefore there are as many local times as there are spaces. It is just as impossible to locate an event in time in an objective way as to locate an object in space in an objective way. Nature is such that it is impossible to measure an absolute velocity by whatever means possible. Nature is concerned only with relative velocities. So you see there is no fixed background of points in space against which a motion can be measured in absolute terms and consequently no absolute flow of time against which an interval of time can be measured.

Experience reveals the strange fluctuations of the sense of time when we approach the same face from different points of views. Time is short during periods of love affairs and long in the painful hours. Therefore, time is not a fact but a relation. Through our mind we break up the spacetime bound and can't get a grip on concepts outside space and time. Therefore, we are in the throes of illusion when we believe ourselves living in the events of present time when no such division really exists. You see the movement of time is within ourselves largely. The quick or slow passing of time is somewhat subjective and its real significance is largely subjective too; mainly in our world of feeling, instead of thinking.

Since this is true (time is concerned with feeling mostly instead of thinking) there is a need for you to take a fresh standpoint to secure a wider and deeper outlook on the relativity of time. The change from the lower to the higher viewpoint, or the shallow to the deeper viewpoint is a matter of insight, for the structure of the world in which we are living depends entirely on the structure of the viewpoint you take. In other words, you see what you are looking for, not what you are looking at. So when you brush away the barrier of what you know as time you know your past lives and your future lives. When you can separate time from your mind and stand off to look at it, without your feelings being affected, you are deathless whether in the flesh or in the spiritual self. This is the meaning of true freedom and the ECK Masters have discovered this secret of life!

More later.

Letters to Gail

May 9, 1963

Dear Gail:

Maya is a force of illusion which leads us to believe in our phenomenal world. It is a Hindu word referring to illusion of the false reality, of seeing something which is actually not there. In other words man is seeing the phenomena instead of the reality of life; the reality being that of God's world.

Maya is a spell of the senses. It is a hypnotic weave of the desire world in which we live, that we see constantly with the five senses; the physical world. This universe is called the prison house of Maya because man has allowed himself to fall out of the audible life stream, and wander about unaided. He thinks and sees all life as material and lets the materialistic guide him instead of the intuitive. Maya puts man in a bondage and holds him there with its alluring song, in the world of sense and matter. It actually is a force made up for the downward pull of man; and faculties of perversions (Kama, Krodha, Lobha, Moha and Ahankara) are the forces or channels it uses to keep one in bondage.

The Isa Upanishads has a line something like this: "Reality is One, but men call It by various names." What is reality? It is that known to orthodox religions as the force of spirit; to science as a field of electro-magnetic force. Maya blinds us to seeing this true field of electrical force which surrounds all, is in all, and above all. Therefore Maya is the illusions of diversity - form, place and time, which are classed by the Orientals under the general term of Maya, illusion, lila or sport. The word Maya signifies the great sea of shadows - the sphere of things as they seem to be as distinguished from a blank sheet of paper which represents one thing and the Reality, the It, as it eternally is. The mothers of the various World Saviors generally bear names derived from the word Maya, as for example, Mary, for the reason that the various redeeming deities signify realization born out of illusion, or wisdom rising triumphant from the tomb of ignorance. Philosophic realization must be born out of the realization of illusion. Consequently the Savior-Gods are born out of Maya and rise through many tribulations into the light of eternity.

For this reason I did the discourse of Time prior to this letter. Time is an illusion when seen in its true form. So are numbers. Numbers partake of the maya of diversity, for they are infinite in their combinations and their progression is limited only by the rational capacity of the mathematician. We find that Pythagoras declared the monad, or the 1, to signify Reality, but the duad, or the 2, illusion. Now it's here that I point out that even the Astral plane is that of illusion, or a Maya world. Here illusion is particularly powerful, and the Astral light which comes to one occasionally is supposedly dangerous for one might believe it is the true spiritual illumination, but are carried to their destruction through it. One falls into a snare and delusion, and the receiver of this light will drift into oblivion in a mystic ecstasy, where fantasy rules.

The ideal of Hinduism is the One Reality, the Brahman. All else is Maya, or illusion. This Reality may take human form as in Krishna; yet in the Inner Shrine looms the vast and awful Vishnu, and the devotee is haunted by the sense of reality. Is not Krishna the maya also? And his activities, are they not lila? However, the central aim of all scriptures is to relate the religious hero to the Eternal, to show how the Eternal is like him, and that his saving grace avails for all who turn to him. All saviors make the staggering claim that "I and my father are one!" Meaning they are the channels through which the power flows. Yet all scriptures appear to lose much of their meaning when we find that the saviors' incarnations are due to maya, or to magic, or to lila. Buddha is claimed to have stepped through the Veil into the earth plane in the scripture called "The Light of Asia," translated by Arnold.

In the Swetasvatara Uphanishad, a savior Rudra-Siva emerges from a background of monistic philosophy and demands bhakti (love) from personal worshippers, and then as if to save the face of the monist, declares the world to be illusion, unreality and maya. Illusion is then the feeling that all that we live in is nothing, and that we are already dead, although imprisoned in a world of senses and matter until the Master or someone is able to release us. The Zen Buddhists say outright to live like one already dead – meaning of course not to live in this world, not take any part in it; exist only because nothing is in harmony with the world except the body, and that is only partially so.

Since this is a warring universe, and everything in it is under attack, including the body, there is nothing one has need for in it. The body is always under attack by bacteria, germs and invisible influences. It is constantly giving away under such attacks—and for that reason the occultists always say, "Be yourself, live in the spirit and let the body go back to the dust." As we eat to please the body, we find that the body is being eaten by bacteria, etc. in order to feed themselves. Not a pleasant thought but nevertheless true. This body is hardly more than a Genetic Entity (G.E.) which is like a growing vegetable and wouldn't have any life, if it wasn't able to trap the spirit of force within itself in order to have movement and action. Otherwise it is hardly worth the time to make its life worth living. There has always been a constant fight against the spirit and matter.

You see Maya is actually the dream world in which you live in that dual viewpoint which sees good and bad. Therefore what is called sin is but an illusion and when the mind or thought are polarized with God, there can be no Maya for you have no illusion. You are beyond good and evil, beauty and ugliness. What causes this blindness to true reality is desire – this puts the veil between us and the Reality. Unattachment breaks through the veil so that nothing stands between the Self and Reality.

The Maya-Desire has two principle functions or powers: (1) Avarana, which veils the eye of reason, blinds it to all but the immediate object of the particular desire, shuts it off from all sense of proportion, of balance, of the truth in the mean. (2) Vikshepa, which flings, or drives or pushes the whole Self (Jivatma) in pursuit of the desired object, to the neglect of all duties. The counteracting, neutralizing, opponents of these two forces are, respectively, the force of Vairagya, which consists of disillusionment, dispassionate, desirelessness, distaste, disgust, with the world. Mujanibat, is that word used of those born of sensitive experience of one's own and much more, of other's miseries, and the persistent pursuit of the Truth.

There is little need for actual suffering in life as the Orthodox religions teach because Maya is the instrument of suffering. Once you can see behind the curtain of Maya and find the true Reality, the world changes. No longer are you able to bear the smallness of life! You are then in position to rise above all the things which make life dull, drab, unbearable and without hope.

More later.

Letters to Gail

May 10, 1963

Dear Gail:

Sometime ago I promised a letter on Depth Psychology. However, this title, which you won't find listed anywhere in library files nor in the psychological listings, is a new terminology for the psychologists. It merely means the study of the subconscious and psychoanalysis.

Sometime ago I wrote a discourse on the Reactive Mind, which is the same as the Subconscious Mind in man. This discourse is a continuation of the Reactive Mind, however I will take up further the study. Both the mind and body of every human functions in two modes. One is the conscious mode; the other is the subconscious. The Conscious Mind expresses the state of awareness when we are awake and when we receive or know we are awake. This part of the mind is presumed to function mainly in the cortex section of the brain. The cortex receives and combines impulses from the eyes, ears, skin and other sensitive structures. These impulses are combined in the cortex creating an overall sensation of being awake, of seeing, hearing, feeling and tasting. It is the objective self which this part of the brain cares for. The process of the Conscious Mind which utilizes the sense organs, is concerned with the present, Here and Now, and serves as a sensitive and highly active lookout station for inner mind, known as the Subconscious or Reactive Mind. This part of the self uses the Conscious Mind as the lookout from time to time, and to make contact with the objective world.

This Reactive Mind or Subconscious Mind has the power to run the body. That is its real function for it is in charge of the sympathetic nervous system (the autonomic nervous system.) Generally it is taught us by religious groups, medical knowledge and other orthodox knowledges that the conscious awareness is the major part of man's being. Formal education, which is that taught to the individual for schooling, college and university work, bases its whole program upon conscious awareness. The subconscious, according to educators, is not recognized, at least that's what the public is told. The western religions call it the 'beast in man.' But as I told you before the Subconscious or the Reactive Mind is that part of the mind which gathers up all the memories, hurts, pains, etc., throughout the life of the entity with which it is attached.

However, the subconscious is a powerful part of the human being, which stands as a barrier between the Conscious Mind and the real Self, Jivatma, Soul, or Superconscious Mind in man. It has an action of its own, but has a one-way channel from the Objective to the Subjective; in other words the Conscious Mind operates a one-way channel to the Subconscious Mind. It will not act unless it has a message from the Conscious Mind; for example, if attacked the Conscious Mind must flash an image to the subconscious so the subconscious can send a message to the body via the nerve channels to go into action. Hence the movement is either to resist or flight. The subconscious does all these things to get the body going without making contact or sending a message back to the Conscious Mind. This is the reason that a person can move swiftly when endangered without conscious thought.

The Subconscious Mind only acts upon images! It receives its messages by images—and in no other way! There is a cooperation between the Conscious Mind and the Subconscious, but many times the Subconscious will not cooperate with the Conscious. There is a reason for this. In our modern so-called civilization we have been entangled purposely or ignorantly (I don't know yet) on the conscious level by thousands of laws, rules and taboos. From infancy we are taught not to do hundreds of things, mainly in the matter of sex. Many of these notions that are so persistently pounded into us are really false and stupid. Some of them are masqueraded under the authority of the holy scriptures, and are harmful to the whole being of man. The present situation concerning the health of the average person is a diabolical notion, for much advertising is persistently aimed at man to show him that he is sick, needs health insurance, needs medical attention, needs surgery, and needs all the drugs on the market. These things, if we accept them by the Conscious Mind, cause it to send these messages to the Subconscious Mind and bring about internal conflict which tends toward despair, illness and death.

Here is where Depth Psychology has its start. Psychology and psychiatry are a part of the medical knowledge used for the curing of the Subconscious mind through psychoanalysis. Also I point out here that the Conscious Mind is the creation of the Subconscious to use as a lookout station in the objective world. The Conscious Mind is a part of the equipment of the Subconscious. Now, the purpose of the Subconscious in creating this instrument called the Conscious Mind was to have it send in correct data (information). Yet if the Conscious Mind sends in false information, then the Subconscious finds itself tricked, deceived and becomes sick. Also it will refuse freely to communicate anything back to the Conscious Mind. So we have a conflict arising in the Subconscious that reflects in the sympathetic nervous system and results in sickness, cancer, abnormal behaviour, crime, etc. So you can say that the majority of our present-day troubles with the individual is that false data is always being fed by the Conscious Mind to the Subconscious, hence it is refusing to answer back directly to the Conscious and the conflict is passed to the nervous system of the body which is responsible for the psychical sense (emotions) – all emotions are results of the physical – chemical – electrical body responses to mental images or pictures created in the Subconscious or Conscious Minds; but mainly the Subconscious – and from these arise the emotions of fear, anger, pain, joy and other states of feeling. Hence the reason why modern advertising uses the picture or symbols to impress the subconscious state of man to arouse desire to purchase products, and the methods of politicians, dictators, and crowd psychology.

The Subconscious is impressed by pictures, images and symbols. It answers back in symbols to the Conscious. This statement alone can explain so much of the language of the mystics, and the methods of our modern life. Remember when I gave you the Reality Scale? Symbolism (which includes pictures and images) was third from top–the first being Knowing, the second is Looking, etc. See, the symbolism which psychologists and religious people class as the top language of God is only a third rate quality.

You see that if the Conscious Mind keeps pounding daily false data into the Subconscious, by those who are already sick, the Subconscious, although resisting false data, will accept and use much of it. And if the data which the Subconscious reluctantly tries to use is false data, then the precise amount that it does accept and try to use, will bring disasterous effects to the individual. Then the individual is informed that he is not following instructions, or obeying the law of God, law of the state or nation, law of humanity, and all the time this is false because the feeder of false data is doing this purposely or non-purposely. This reaction of the Subconscious Mind to false data has gained a name called the Law of Retribution, by the psychologists, the Law of Cause and Effect by the occultists, the Law of Karma by the orientals, the Law of Compensation in physics, and the Law of Justice by the jurisprudence. In Christianity it is the Law of Moses or Law of Balance.

The Subconscious is then a mirror which reflects that which the senses give it, plus the messages sent to the body. Hence you see it is not a spiritual study, but a lower study of the mind and body of the human being. This is why hypnotism works, why sending messages to the Subconscious Mind for improvement in health, money, etc., works. Hence, you can see the foundation for Christian Science, Unity, New Thought, Orthodox religions, Communism, political parties and a few other hundred organized institutions which try to tell man that it is the proper one for the individual. You can now see why ideas rule, and not the individual. You can see why one person is stronger than another, because he can set up picture images in other minds and pound them home.

One last thought. The Subconscious Mind will act upon the right images and messages if given to it. But they must be consistent and powerful, positive, beneficient and constructive messages. It not only accepts these messages but will act upon them at once!

More later.

Letters to Gail

May 11, 1963

Dear Gail:

Every society produces at least some members who are personally ambitious men who are more highly motivated than their fellows. A personally ambitious person is seldom, however, one who makes a creative contribution to the development of society. Ordinarily he accepts things as they are and simply endeavors in socially conventional ways to improve his position within the existing social context. He may do this by working harder than most, by being more ruthless, or by trickery and deceit.

The more successful of such men have from time to time won great wealth and power; and many are remembered as historically important princes, kings, generals, popes, conquerors, dictators. It is men of this sort who in the modern world are acclaimed in the headlines and are reputed to be the shapers of human destiny. They do stand out above their fellows; but they seldom contribute to the making of enduring and significant social changes.

So be not deceived by history, biography, present-day newspapers, events and loose talk. The man who makes some change, however slight, in his society, does so through endeavor of an original, rather than conventional sort. He is not simply more industrious, more determined, more ruthless, or more skilled in some traditional art or craft than the majority of men; he is more active – mentally or physically – and this man is distinctive in that he has both high motivation and initiative; and this latter attribute would seem to be the result of socially produced detachment from, or discontent with, some aspect of society plus a socially atypical faith in his own acumen. For unless a person believes that he is in his own right superior to the authority of custom, convention, tradition, and the people who embody that authority – father, king, or priest – he will be unlikely to apply himself to improve upon what they represent.

For this very reason you will be unhappy with the times, people and the world in which you are living, once all the knowledge of the occult or spiritual has started flowing your way. Already you are showing an attitude without knowing, nor of your own conscious volition, that you are fitting into the above statement. Look now, the real changers of history are those whom we admired greatly: Jesus, Buddha, St. Paul,

Mohammed, and others. St. Paul is a good example of a man who couldn't abide the society of the Greeks in his day and therefore he completely changed a society which was foreign to him. So did Bodhidharma, the Buddhist who went to China, from India, in about the 6th century. You see the power of an idea, propagated by mouth or pen, is far stronger than the sword. Napoleon was a great conqueror, remembered historically. But what did he do for society? – nothing. About all you can say about him is – he was a landlord who got his property by the sword.

The man of mental activity is generally one who will go along with social customs, and accept things as they are, and try to improve his position in the existing social order. But a man of spiritual activity is induced by the social circumstances, the distrust of social authority, to greater individual confidence in himself and to undertake to work a change in his society. It is evident that by doing this the man of spiritual activity sets himself apart from ordinary men, and his faith in his endeavor is amazing. He must have this abundance of faith for hardly will society accept his idea until it has proven itself. Ideas are therefore the most powerful weapons of all.

Therefore any man who sets out to make his idea accepted in a society must have both great and enduring faith in his own judgment and skills and a large amount of contempt for the opinion of his fellows. This is proven throughout the whole time track of man, in discoverers, inventors, developers. They all struggled long and suffered many failures, and they have been ignored, persecuted before they achieved their self-set goals. Nevertheless, it has been just rare and atypical men – Columbus, Karl Marx, Fubbi Quantz, Martin Luther, Jacob Boehme, St. Peter, and hundreds of others – who worked the changes that made our society today more fruitful than that of the past centuries.

This makes for the fact that 99.999% of people you meet are ordinary. Hardly anybody has an ambition for improving his position in society. The Protestant Ethic says that man earns his way into heaven by being energetic, accumulating materials, and by being enterprising. The slothful, unambitious and the ignorant will not make it, and nobody within the Protestant success framework wants any part of them. You find this true among the Presbyterians, Methodists, Episcopalians, and the Baptists. The Catholics reverse the doctrine by pointing out that this earthly life is hard, suffering, etc., and that man will be rewarded in heaven for partaking in it. But those individuals who believe in neither of these points are on the outside of pale as far as the society in America goes. Generally an individual must have his own social life, his economic life among the ethical group with which he belongs. America was formed by those who proclaimed such freedom but it doesn't work out that way.

Briefly, the Protestant Ethic creed in this country is an offshoot of the old New England Puritan Founders. Hard work, ambition, orthodoxy and enterprise are the basic points infused into their religious creed which was for the times under which they lived, but which are still today the basic postulates in our social, business and economic life. It is a part of the education drilled into the children in grade school, and through all grades including college. This comes back to the point that ideas are weapons. And before I forget, the Capitalistic system was built upon the Protestant Ethic creed, which was long in use before it reached the shores of this country, but in the U.S. it has reached its zenith.

What has this got to do with the subject of spirituality? It is a yardstick by which you measure the lower against the higher. The Protestant Creed, the Catholic Creed, and Buddhist Creed – all under the present interpretation are materialistic and have no place in the spiritual life. This goes for Dr. Norman Vincent Peale's doctrine also. But they are ideas which in the war between religious groups have gained converts. It is amazing how ideas stick in the minds of the audience. But what I am saying is when a man of spiritual activity starts out to preach his idea to the world he tends to change the social structure of the society in which he lives. He is what you might call an earth-mover! Confucious can certainly be called an earth-mover, for he changed the face of China for centuries. Valmiki, author of Ramayana, India's sacred poem of 48,000 verses is also an earth-mover; Lai Tsi, Mary Baker Eddy, Zoroaster, Nietzsche, Florence Nightingale, Jalal-din-Rumi, Shamus-I-Tabriz, Thomas Aquinas, Levasseur, Lenin, John Wesley, and others.

An earth-mover hardly meets with approval of society for he is changing the customs and ways of that society. Society doesn't want to be changed, the individual wants to stay as he is. He is safe, secure in his little niche in life. But as you go along in your study you will find the comparison I've made coming true with what you discover.

More later.

May 12, 1963

Dear Gail:

The subject this time is "Space." The frank realization that the physical science is concerned with the world of shadows is one of the most significant advances in modern physics whose real beginning was made by the theory of relativity.

Space means nothing apart from our perception of objects, and time means nothing apart from our experience of events. Space started merely as fiction created by man's own mind; an illegitimate extension to nature of a subjective concept which helps to understand and describe the arrangements of objects seen by man, while time appears as a second fiction serving a similar purpose for the arrangement of events which happen to man. Time and space are both maya in modern physics and philosophy. The frames of space and time are relative. Distance, volumes, all quantities of space and time reckoning which belong to these frames are also relative.

Einstein's law has proved itself the better that the quest of the Absolute is the best way to understand relative appearances. Any knowledge of the eternal world cannot be divorced from the nature of any appliances with which we obtain knowledge. Any knowledge of laws of this universe can't be regarded as subsisting apart from the experimental procedure by which we have ascertained truth. Try putting yourself in the center of nothingness without anchor points, and you're lost.

Here are some of the points to remember about the Theory of Relativity: (1) A straight line is not necessarily straight. (2) A ray of light has weight. (3) Space is curved. (4) The universe is boundless and yet finite. (5) Mind creates matter and matter creates space. (6) Each Jivatma constructs its own universe. (7) Space and Time are not realities. There is no fundamental entity called space existing in itself in which the world is placed nor is there any fundamental line in which an event occurs. Hence the ECKist in seeking nothingness is seeking the truth – where Christianity must still hold to the mind concept of a heaven, a space created by the mind. ECKANKAR goes beyond space, into the void. Christianity is therefore a religion of the mind – not of spiritual reality. So you see that out of an observer's temporal experience we construct observed time and out of the same time measures we observe space. Thus the universe and with it, if we observe closely, its creator is neither in space nor time. The shortest straight line is an infinite affair and the universe is infinitesimally small. Therefore atoms are world systems and world systems are atoms. The mind of man is truly omnipresent because all time and space is present in it – but God is not omnipresent, as the scriptures claim, because time and space are not in Him. (Check the fifth plane and above in Tiger's Fang.) Space, time and the physical world of substances have no objective reality, apart from the mental concepts of them that man creates in his mind. Nothing is real except what is in our consciousness and perception. It is only when we view ourselves in space and time that we are quite obviously distinctive individuals. When we pass beyond space and time we form ingredients of a continuous stream of light (see Tiger's Fang as reference.)

The individual is responsible for building his own universe within the universe, and he is responsible for making the universe what it is. We use the building materials of space, time and illusions. We put them together consciously or unconsciously with our applied knowledge of superficial education in a career, trade or work, using those measuring devices I spoke about earlier. We work within a framework of time and space, and we spend our off hours from work in a framework of time and space. Even dreaming is within the same references of this framework.

An event has many sizes relative to its corresponding standpoints. There are as many imaginary worlds as observers with varying interests and purpose and these worlds appear to change in accordance with the subjective changes in the life of those who experience them. When we discard our human viewpoint entirely we find that light and sound are neither waves nor particles, neither is God the Master or Himself, but has the nature of both. The nature of light and sound is such they behave as waves in empty space but like bullets as soon as it (light and sound) encounters matter. Thus we are, in the world of matter, concerned then with giving space to others.

I am speaking in the field of psychic space. If you allow another person psychic space then he will be free around you and able to express himself ably. But once you close in on his psychic space he can hardly breathe. For example, a wife who corrects her husband constantly, calls him at the office on little things to do for her, won't let him have an evening away from her, is crowding his psychic space and choking him. Two results are forthcoming: (1) He can or will leave her and find someone who won't crowd him so closely – take up his psychic space, or (2) Be destroyed by her, or destroy her by physical violence. This question of psychic space giving is so important to the human existence. You understand that you carry your own universe with you, and once you allow someone to enter that universe, beware that they don't crowd their space (or universe) into yours. I've often wondered why the psychologists do not know more about this.

You've experienced the feeling when somebody is on the telephone, or enters into your presence whose being seems to push, shove or crowd you uncomfortably. They have either pulled you into their universe, or entered yours and are crowding you too closely. Aggressive people are of this nature, and abuse the beingness of another person too strongly. I'll take up the subject of making space, giving space and beingness in another letter.

Our measurements are never of space and time but only of the things and the events that occupy space and time. My time measurements depend utlimately on my space measurements and the latter depend on my ideas of simultaneous relations with these qualities. Therefore the same world appears different to different observers. Therefore, every observer lives in his own imaginary world. As in a dream-experience, earth, roads, mountains denote only forms of empty space, so in the waking experience also they are forms of empty space, depending on the position of the observer. I, you, he or she are also imaginary forms of waking experience. When one becomes awake the dream is destroyed; the condition of self-realization destroys the waking completely, because the Jivatma realizes at last that all sense-matter is a dream, and awareness objectively is nothing but false reality.

Since language is based on old concepts we can't give or get a satisfactory explanation of the sense-matter dream or objective awareness. Therefore understanding in the world of matter means nothing except familiarity and accustomedness.

More later.

Letters to Gail

May 14, 1963

Dear Gail:

Briefly I want to point out the subtle current going on in this country. The individual doesn't count anymore. Take for example the business tactics: the executives and the employees exist for the good of the business and as individuals they simply don't count – this is true of society as a whole. If the individual cannot exist for the good of society he is therefore a beatnik, a square peg, an outcast to society.

If this be the thesis of our society it is also the thesis of Soviet Communism. There is hardly a hair between western society and communistic society. There is hardly an existing hair's breadth between Catholicism and communism, or Brahamism, nor true Buddhism, nor any European society as it exists today – and this includes the dictators. There is the same overdriving of the individual to get that utmost efficiency out of him for the benefit of the firm, the state, society, government, or whatever you choose to call it, the same instantly ruthless discarding of him the moment he begins to weaken, the same contempt for the individual as a person, and reward and admiration of him only as a tool of some vague purpose which in our country seems to be the making of a lot of money for big corporations and their stockholders, in Russia for the protection of their state; and in society there are those same false values which apparently everybody wants for prestige and honors. In the church it appears to be the need of trying for a reward in the hereafter – whatever it is – the result is a reward until one gets too old to struggle for the reward.

So you see the basic philosophy underlying big business, the communist state, our existing society, here and elsewhere – in fact the whole civilization – is exactly the same. In Russian society when you slip a little you get shot or sent to a forced prison camp. In our society (western) your resignation is asked for, or else you are forced to give it without being asked through humiliation beyond endurance. The church flips you in with a guilt burden which is beyond any conception.

What I am trying to say here is this: Individualism is gone! One is no longer able to be free for pressures are put upon him constantly to be something else, not himself! In our department store society we are given everything on an assembly line, or a supermarket style. It reminds me of what a priest said about his own people and church. Church, according to him, was now like a supermarket – the members could come on Sunday, and while mass was going on, confess, listen to the sermon, take part in the mass, and get communion, within 45 minutes. True, but so is all life today – listen to any normal person talk and his talk has no sense to it, rambling, no ideas of depth, superficial, and boastful! Everything is generally what he has read and then it was digested, if at all, carelessly!

My basic idea for this letter now comes into focus. First, I want to discuss that type of person who is labeled the People Pleaser. Secondly, I will discuss the type of person known as the Fear Merchant. I gave you the background against which these basic types work as a pattern. But what has this got to do with spiritual or occult study?

I am giving you yardsticks by which to go in the judgment of people whose attitudes you meet in daily life; the doctor, priest, lawyer, student, teacher, bus driver, etc. Their profession means nothing, it is how they meet life, and this will be your own success with the spiritual life; by looking at others and determining their methods in meeting problems you can either avoid or learn for yourself. This is actually the development of that quality of discrimination within yourself – and frankly, this leads to non-attachment.

People Pleasers are those who feel that they must at all times please others. This is the Dale Carnegie type, the salesman, the merchant, the type of person who is emotionally maladjusted so badly that he must give his all to serve the public. There is a difference in doing things to serve the public and trying to please the public. Usually a People Pleaser is one who is loaded with fear of (1) losing his job, (2) of hurting other people's feelings, (3) of trying too hard, and usually ending up getting hurt himself, (4) of being too shy and timid to actually say what he thinks. Any person can speak his mind, with force, if the occasion justifies it, and yet not hurt others' feelings, but cause a respect for himself for saying it. In fact, I've seen professional people have such little confidence in themselves that they would whisper the charge for their service rather than speak up confidently and forthrightly. I had a doctor who was of this nature – and my respect for him diminished so swiftly I dropped him, for he kept me on the edge with his effeminate mannerisms and I was constantly on the defense to please him.

Letters to Gail

A People Pleaser is not a happy person, because he can't speak his mind without feeling that he is going to hurt somebody's feelings, and have anger thrown at him. In fact he is a very common type in our society, and he constantly edges around the crowd so that he can be a part of it, yet he wants to stand outside so he won't be stepping on toes.

The Fear Merchant is that sort of person who wants to control you by playing upon your nerves and fears. So many of our people in this society have been conditioned to either listen to their mothers, who were Fear Merchants warning junior what would happen if he disobeyed mother, or grown aggressive in the fact that almost everything mother said proved to be false. But a Fear Merchant is one who is constantly telling you what is good for you, and if you fail to do what he wants, dire results are going to happen. Common results they predict are: losing your job, losing friends, losing your money, losing prestige, losing out in the race of life, going to hell, creating the big sin, being destitute and broke, finding troubles, ending up in jail, getting with child, trouble with police, and all sorts of little goodies.

Their homilies are similar to B. Franklin's, "Early to bed and early to rise makes one healthy, wealthy and wise." They love to give sermons on the negative side of life, warnings, predictions, and threats, even making their point with anecdotes of what happened to their friends who didn't take their advice! According to their philosophy hardly anything you do is right – but they have the right answer, right religion, right advice, right work. One of their favorite expressions is: "I know that I'm just a poor, uneducated sort of person, but what you are doing isn't right!" This false humility is for the birds! It's a lever to throw you! There is also the direct, aggressive type who won't hesitate to tell you that they are the world's best and you are inferior, so do it their way!

Remember, a Fear Merchant, as well as a People Pleaser is an angry person. Neither have self-confidence or they wouldn't be using this sort of behavior. It is actually a herd instinct or behavior pattern. But compare this with those persons whose behavior is opposite – who are not (1) A People Pleaser, and (2) A Fear Merchant! Those who will help if asked, give advice only from their own experience – and grant you beingness or psychic space. Both types 1 and 2 are those who crowd your psychic space – and now you should be able to manage them, or avoid completely.

More later.

May 15, 1963

Dear Gail:

The subject is Beingness. Being is existence, conscious existence of something, as things brought into being by projection. It is that which exists as an actuality or entity in time or space, in idea or matter; also, that which is logically conceivable and hence capable of existence. It is the fullness of life or perfection possible to a thing that exists: as, being is the end of becoming.

So the conclusion of this definition was: being is the end of becoming! This is the part in which we are most interested! Being is often substituted for survival, and vice-versa – that is survival of the Jivatma. This is actually summed up in the two words – To Be! Being does not depend upon the physical universe and, in fact, it is lessened by participation in the physical universe. Thus we speak of survival after death – meaning of course, Being. We can separate the Being of the Jivatma as spirit from its survival in the physical universe.

The Jivatma and the infinity can meet in an identity as one and the same thing, by the Jivatma acting in the capacity To Be! This depends upon the opposing scales of attitude – To Be and Not To Be. The high and the low, and the degree of attitude along, or between these opposites depends upon the Jivatma. The extreme opposites of this scale, are as thus: When the Jivatma is in the To Be level, it is at oneness with spirit, and when in the Not-To-Be-level, it is at oneness with the physical universe. Hence the existence of illusion or maya, in the latter level, as pointed out in the letter on Maya. When in this state it is one of non-participation, or non-creating level, a non-survival state. Hence the term hell, which means a non-creating state. Whenever an individual is failing To Be, he is also failing to exist in some capacity, or reversing himself to a low level in the negative state of being.

One of the chief aspects of negative and positive Being is the aspect of Cause and Effect. When an individual is Cause, he is Being positively. When he is Effect he is Being negatively. Naturally this is concerned with psychic space, for the more beingness an individual possesses the larger psychic space he needs. So life itself and all its randomity consists of beingness and whether it wants you to have beingness. So all things have beingness and all life is beingness. The ants have been granted beingness but do not have beingness itself. The Jivatma can have beingness anywhere – it can go down under sea and up in the clouds; that is the beingness it is granted for motion. All things including living things have been granted a certain beingness itself. But once you start interfering with the communication line that monitors a line of living things like animals, or insects, you will find something getting awfully angry at you.

The material things can't have ideas, but life can by granting beingness to something that has given it life. A Jivatma can grant an unlimited amount of beingness to anything, but he can do this as long as he doesn't resist beingness in return. For example, no angry person can grant you beingness, for he wants to control your body and mind, and control doesn't give you beingness (meaning freedom in this case! or in other words the right to be yourself!). Therefore when he refuses another the right to be himself – he also refuses himself beingness! This is the racial problem; by refusing to grant beingness to the minority the majority cuts off its own beingness. When you have a lack of freedom it means you have not granted yourself the right to be yourself! This means you are cutting off your own psychic space. Understand?

Anyone who does grant beingness to a town, person or nation will in turn be granted beingness, kindness and generosity. This is apparently one of the ways that the law works. The less beingness you grant anything lesser the less will be given to yourself. This is true especially in larger groups and those low on the tone scale – but the higher one goes on the tone scale, the more beingness he grants to others and the more he receives in return.

The fight between sexes is actually this granting of beingness. That is one sex refuses to grant beingness to the other. So if one doesn't grant beingness to anyone whom he is communicating with, he will eventually begin to fight the willingness to grant beingness to all things. If one refuses or resists granting beingness he will be attacked by that which he has refused to grant beingness. This action will force him into less and less space – psychic space – and after a while he will suffocate with the problem of a lack of space – this being true it is a problem of the individual working against himself. But you generally find anyone doing this will invariably blame somebody else or something for their own problems. It is an introversion of their minds, and by looking at themselves, they fail to see what is wrong, or don't wish to and place the blame elsewhere. It is that old story – never take responsibility for one's own actions, but hand them to somebody else. In the west it seems that to shift blame is a common ailment.

Among those who wish to control others the granting of beingness is a crime; for example, look at Hitler. He couldn't grant beingness to the Jews because it would take away his own controls, so he thought. This was a case of granting too much beingness to one group and not enough to another. Any argument is simply the basic fact that one will not grant the other beingness to something or to each other. If one can grant beingness to himself, and he is resisted, then he won't grant beingness to others. This is always the making of small or large dictators or those who gain power through control of the masses be it by rule of law or by force of arms.

One can develop very heavy somatic problems by the refusal of granting beingness to others. If one becomes introverted he can develop somatic problems (i.e., body pains, body ailments; example: migraine headaches, toothaches, feet hurting, pains and ailments caused from emotional charges, etc.) which are caused by the attention being drawn to one's own self. If you want sensations all you have to do is to declare that the sensation has a greater beingness than you have, and that you want the energy that the sensation creates– and that it does happen. If you create sensation in order to get sensation, you will get a superiority of beingness above you that isn't your own, in whatever you are creating the sensation in. But working with wave lengths as this is – you are to be careful for wave lengths with inanimate objects are not as troublesome as working with humans whose wave lengths can be stuck with yours in the same band you're working within, and the granting can expand or close the energy band in which you are established at that time.

Any writer or artist who won't grant beingness to his work is a very bad creative worker. The more that a writer has to do with facts, or an artist in the same category, the more of a hack they are. An artist must grant beingness to his paintings, a writer to his writings, etc. This beingness is an aliveness, that which shakes with energy. One is alive as much as he is willing to grant beingness to others, all things. No artificial stimulant or love affair will grant him anything more than his willingness of granting beingness to all things.

More later.

Letters to Gail

May 17, 1963

Dear Gail:

Tonight we talk about cults. Before getting into the subject I have a couple of things to point out. First, I want to give a thought on the doctrines which prevail in our times. First, the Catholic doctrine – it says that man is guilty of the original sin and cannot succeed to salvation, until he enters the church; The Protestant Ethic says that man is a moral failure and cannot succeed here and now unless he adopts the Protestant creed; Christian Science says that man is sick and cannot be healed unless he adopts the C.S. moral creed; Freudian doctrine says man is shackled by his biological urges that can never be freely expressed and which put him in conflict with his society; Marxianism (that which the communists have adopted) is a doctrine of social destiny in which man must play the role of a passive functionary in his society. It claims that man is an animal and cannot rise above his state in life, except when his fellow man also rises.

This leads us into the Cults. You will find the above will give you a better insight into the cults — A cult is a system of worship of a deity. It is great devotion to some person, idea, or thing, especially when such devotion is viewed as an intellectual fad. It can be called a sect. One thinks of a cult being bad – especially do the laymen in a religious group like the churches with large congregations. Cults are like anything else, they can be good, bad and indifferent – usually the mystery schools are cults. You can call the Aquarian Foundation a cult, Scientology is one, Worship of Bal (in old Bible), Mithra, Osiris, Zeus, Adonis, etc. The latter ones were some of the earliest cults known in history. In modern times we have had the political cults, worship of Hitler, Worship of Mussolini, Worship of Stalin, etc. In this country we had the worship of public figures in movies, politics, etc. making the movement a cult.

There are a number in this country which I'll briefly give you. They are: Psychiana, a movement started by Frank Robinson, Moscow, Idaho, 1928. He advertised that he talked with God, and you could too. His work was all correspondent courses for which one paid a pretty penny. His death revealed that he had the largest mailing list of its kind in the country – died in 40's. Father Divine's Peace Mission Movements. I don't know what he teaches except for the colored people to be of peaceful nature, work hard and stay together. He has been successful in making good citizens out of his followers – which are about 30 million, I'm told. I went to one of his banquets – interesting. New Thought, a movement started in England in 1890 by Judge Thomas Toward. It has a mixed theory of revelation which says spirit is the guiding, healing and moving force in man's life, and man can be anything he desires. It's a hodgepodge of theosophy, positivism, protestanism, freudianism, and christian science. Eighteen different groups have adopted New Thought theories for their own, each making claims that they are original. Some of them are: Unity Church of Truth; Institute of Religious Science; Divine Science; Church of Healing Christ, Radiant Life Fellowship, etc. Christian Science is a stable cult, which believes moral life will bring healing of the sick; Theosophy believes in the main Buddhistic and Brahmanic theories with pantheistic ladder of Gods and reincarnation. The I Am movement, founded by Edna Ballard, is a group based upon the fact that man doesn't know he is endowed with divine authority, and what he thinks and feels comes into form. Liberal Catholic church, an offshoot of the Roman Catholic Church, founded in 1870 by Von Dollinger, in Holland. It refuses to accept the doctrine of infallibility of pope. It has been tied with theosophy in the past through its leaders. Has adopted much of the theosophical theories. Spiritualism – a theory of religion which claims control with spirits beyond this world, through mediums. Andrew Jackson Davis was one of the best in this field. Swedenborg, the Swede, founded his church of New Jerusalem on spiritualism. There are several summer camps over the country; the best known is Lily Dale in New York; Chesterfield in Indiana, where the spiritualists gather during the summer months. Some educators who have worked in this field are: Wm James, Harvard, James Hyslop, Columbia University, Morton Prince, Princeton University, Dr. Rhine, Duke University. The Jehovah's Witnesses deny their movement is religious. They claim religion is contrary to the will of God, and belongs to the devil. Their theory is that God is to come one of these days and turn the earth into a garden spot, where everybody will live happily, forever! Of course their warning is negative for it is based upon destruction of evil and what happens to he who doesn't live the good life now! His reward will be nil! The Oxford Movement known as Buchmanism, or Moral Rearmament is a group of people who have been converted to do-gooders. Belief is moral righteousness, public confession and group guidance. Mormonism is a group who follows the dictates of the angels who spoke to Joseph Smith, 1843. There are the usual moral codes, belief in returning to this earth in material form for eternity and happiness, the domination of male principle, and industry among its people as a society. Four Square Gospel, Aimee McPherson, founder, in L.A., who believed in divine healing and a hellfire-damnation gospel to toast her audience's feet. The Baha'i Faith is a group founded by the Bab, executed in 1844, in Persia. It is an offshoot of Moslem – and the Bab, a Persian name for Christ, was Mirza Muhammad Ali, who came as the messenger of God, for the conversion of the world. There is a huge temple devoted to this faith in Wilmette, Ill., just above Chicago. Its belief is that Baha'i will someday be the universal religion of the world, and are working toward the cause. It's belief is one God, moral life, reincarnation, love, and eternity for those who succeed in working out their karma. One can be a good Baha'ist and belong to an orthodox church.

Of course there are many others. The Millerites, Snake Handlers of Tennessee, Hutterite, Penitente, The Vedantist, Self-Realization Church, Anglo-Israel Church, Quakers, Chapel of Truth, Unitarians, Dukhobors, Shakers, Mind Institute of Los Angeles, Quimbyism, Rosicrucians, Dianetics, Ontological Society, United Brethren, Church of Astral Light, Voodooism, and a half-hundred others that you should know about and will in the course of your studies come across. You can always recognize them by their sales pitch – which is generally: "Follow my methods and you will be able to have anything in life you wish!" When asked if there are any charges, the answer is always no, but there is a love offering, and that is generally a large sum named which is always given. You can always recognize their generalities – for none can get down to any specifics. One of their methods is the old Father John pitch — that is saying that Mr. Jones, who is a prominent man (but maybe you've never heard of him) was healed of a dangerous disease, or made a lot of money following the advice of the cult leader.

One of the other ways of recognizing these pseudo-religious groups, is their emphasis upon evil – that man is possessed of hatred and evil and they can exorcise this out of man, if only allowed. If one fails after following their instructions it is never that anything is wrong with the Cult and its teachings, but with the individual who has not cast out evil yet. And so forth.

More later.

Letters to Gail

May 18, 1963

Dear Gail:

Magicians are strange creatures. They have two paths to follow – the right hand path which is the white magic or good magic and the left hand path which is the black magic or bad magic. There is no center or middle path as one might call it.

A magician is not especially interested in reaching the goal of being one with the deity which is the final path of the mystics. He is concentrated on learning the techniques of manipulating the forces of nature. He works with nature and over nature to gain his ends; the white magician is working for the good of universal mankind and the black magician is working for himself. These are the end goals of each type. A magician might be called a necromancer, sorcerer, a conjurer. However, he deals with the secret forces of nature and works in the astral plane where the spiritual force is a dualistic nature. Hence the reason why he can use either the negative or the positive forces.

Magicians work on a mental level, using the mind powers for their illusions, phenomena and healings. They can be witchdoctors, kahunas, priests, mediums, shamans, medical doctors, or that which we know today as advertising men, propagandists, etc. They work with a principle called vital force, which is known to us as Soul force, and which is existent in man, animal, plant. Sometimes this is called mana and can be manipulated so that phenomena occurs, such as the raising of tables; moving furniture without apparent human effort; levitation; making a change in the weather; and the holding of life and death in the hands of a single person.

Many groups use magic today but it is, under another name, still as primitive as the earlier days in our history of mankind. Magic went undercover when the orthodox religious groups came into power, when medicine gained a political hold over people, when science became a popular fad trying to explain away the mysteries of mind and nature. Voodoo still practices its magic in many parts of the world, including civilized London and America. The witch doctor is prominent among the South American Indians, negro tribes in Africa, and the Shaman is popular with the peoples of the north. All these were very necessary before the invention of psychology and psychoanalysis. You must understand that with the advent of the industrial revolution, the social revolution and the leisure which man is gaining today, the church lost its hold over the masses, and Luther's schism brought a new power into office, the industrialist has needed all the resources possible to keep the people in check. So it is done through several agencies, not as an organized plan but one which has fitted in, hand and glove together.

Man was once a God who walked the earth, but now he is reduced to being a puppet who is enslaved to work for the benefit of others. The Freudian doctrine which has been accepted by our western civilization has set forth a theory that man is inherently weak, that he must be mothered from childhood to death by his mother and, when he is old enough, married to a woman who will take over where mother departed. The old theory under which we lived until the advent of Freudism was that too much mothering made a boy a weakling. This new doctrine (comparatively new – 50 years old) has brought about the conflicts seen in our society today, where youth won't take discipline; hence the juvenile problems. It is practiced in the Catholic church – although this would be denied if questioned – but if you stop to think about how much emphasis is put upon the Mother of God by the church, then you can start thinking what is behind all this. This thought has taken over our whole life in society today.

Where does this fit in with magic? The Freudian doctrine is the antithesis of magic, as well as is the church. In the east where magic is practiced daily by all peoples from high government officials to peasantry, the Brahmans (priest caste) tried the same controls over people as the church did from its beginning in Rome by putting together a doctrine which says that man is weak, an animal, and lives at the mercy of a creator who deals only through its priests. Magic, on the other hand, created Gods of men, when it was white magic; when black magic it tried to reduce men to zero points. Get the point? This being true, then the orthodox religions, psychoanalysis, medicine, etc., are practicing black magic today – that is to some extent. At least this is my thought because they are trying to make controls on man through moral and materialistic laws.

Some of the greatest magicians known in history have been: Count Alessandro Cagliostro, Hermes Trismegistos, Apollonius of Tyanna, Albert Magnus, Agrippa of Nettesheim, Adonis, Mesmer, Paracelsus, Plotinus, Simon Magus, William Butler Yeats, etc. These men are the ancestors of many today who walk the streets unknown to others as magicians. A magician has power over the fire elementals, water elementals, wind elementals and earth elementals. Western magic stems from earlier civilizations – the Chaldean, Babylonian, Assyrian, Greek and Roman. The Jewish people took it up and developed it in the cabala to the high form of what it is today. Palestine was the crossroads in the early days when the Romans learned of it during their occupation of the city and took much back to Italy, thus spreading it to the rest of the western world.

The Essenes was a Jewish cult, to which Jesus belonged, that trained its members in magic. It was one of the early mystery schools. It was put on paper for the first time in 12th century in Spain and later picked up in Poland by a mystery school (as Chassidism) where a famous rabbi taught it. Later a German monk put down the secret science in a manuscript after being initiated into a secret order of magicians, and started a secret school in his homeland, the first except for the Knight Templars who practiced magic until destroyed by the King of France in the 16th century. Elphas Levi belonged to the German school, but he revealed his findings in an amazing set of books which can be found in certain libraries over the country. His works revived a group who in the last century opened the famous Order of Golden Dawn to which belonged a number of writers: Wm. Butler Yeats, Alistair Crowley, Arnold Bennett, A.E. Waite, etc.

Much of Jung's, the psychologist, works belong to the secret teachings of magic. Anyway, the secret wisdom teaches that man's destiny is in his own hands, that he is a God, he can control the powers of his mind. Some of the secrets are too powerful to divulge except to the purest initiate. In the course of time the student of magic learns telepathy; healing of insanity, drunkeness, disease; how to project his desires into the formative world where all things must originate before materialization; learns to control spiritual forces by symbols, by rituals and by divination; learns the art of clairvoyance and clairaudience. He learns astral travelling and about other planes where he can travel by his other bodies. He learns the Tattwa vision and the Tattwa tides. His powers of concentration, memory, intuition, creative imagination and judgment are enormously increased.

More later.

Letters to Gail

May 19, 1963

Dear Gail:

The subject is "Exoteric and Esoteric Knowledge." Definitions of these terms are: Exoteric – that knowledge which is exterior, external, that knowledge suitable to be imparted to the public. Esoteric – that knowledge which is designed for and understood by the specially initiated alone; abstruse, also, belonging to the circle initiated in such teachings; that which is withheld from open avowal; private teachings with a purpose.

I won't concern you with exoteric knowledge, the knowledge gained from formal education, but with esoteric teachings. While exoteric teachings have a way of coming to an end eventually, sometimes when the mind has taken all it wants for a lifetime, and concerns itself with games, the esoteric knowledge abides in perpetual learning, always in equilibrium with life. The esoteric knowledge is never given in public lectures – usually in private – often they appear as public talks but the nature of their attraction will not bring many to the lecturer. Plato says, "A wise man is one capable of correctly estimating the extent not only of his own knowledge or ignorance but also of performing the same service for others." No one is wise who is not as fully acquainted with the extent of ignorance as with the extent of wisdom; for in mortal concerns wisdom is an inconsequential area of rationality existing in an infinite expanse of ignorance.

It is Socrates who infers that wisdom is not the knowledge of things but the knowledge of the condition of knowledge with respect to its absence or presence; an observation plainly intimating that wisdom deals with generals and not particulars. Wisdom may therefore be considered as composed of universals of knowing and the sciences of the particulars of knowing, which as the practical are suspended from theory. Exoteric knowledge then is the knowledge of particulars, a familiarity with those arts and sciences arrived at through application and concentration on external natures. Esoteric knowledge is concerned with the inherent nature of knowledge itself, and is limited to those acquainted with the more profound issues of philosophy and the sublime mysteries of life.

The esoteric teachings are given through mystery schools or individual teachings. The latter you are receiving. Every orthodox religion has its esoteric teachings, which the orthodox ministry doesn't want to be exposed to the congregation. First, because many priests do not know nor want to consider esoteric teachings as a part of the religious body. Second, because esoteric teachings do not fit man into the pattern of his society – it separates him from the masses and he becomes an outsider, a cliffhanger, an eccentric. Our society is a department store and supermarket society which has its chief creative center in the Great Lakes region – Chicago, Milwaukee, Minneapolis, etc. The salesman or shopkeeper who objects to the ruthlessness of the Russians is the person who sees no limit to enslaving poor people by selling them things on installment plan at outrageous rates of interest, which the poor person can't understand.

Science, today, claims it has overthrown the false gods and dogmas of creed, but the mysteries of the divine spheres elude the grasp of corporeal learning since they belong to a more subtle and esoteric realm. The mysteries hold the true keys to wisdom. They are the custodians of the secrets more arcane. Who were the leaders in the mystery schools? Pythagoras, Plato, Aristotle, Socrates, Sanchuniathon, Porphyry, Cicero, Epictetus, Tulsi Das, Guru Nanak, Rumi, etc. I named only the westerners and a couple of orientals. There are hundreds of others. The mystery schools are: Gnostics, Druids, White Brotherhood, Mithra, Cabala, Yoga Satsang, Magi, Zen Buddhism and Sufi, to name a few. The esoteric side of the orthodox religions are: Protestantism – Masons; Catholicism – Knights of Columbus (I think – I don't know any other group); Buddhism – Zen and Tibetan-type Buddhism; Hinduism – a large number like Sri Aurobindo, followers of Upanishads; Confucianism – Taoist; Islam – Sufi; Judaism – the Zoharists and Cabalists.

One note to point out: The western religions are theistic – meaning a belief in one God; the Oriental, pantheistic, meaning several gods in one belief. Now when one begins to see behind the illusions of life, "veil after veil is torn away from the inner (spiritual) eye until at last it gazes upon the final mystery." Thus the seeker comes to the goal of all life! But when? I don't know this answer. I could be very deft in giving a smug answer in that it is when the individual sets his determination. It is determination, will and employment of concentration, for these are faculties of the Jivatma, not the mind. The mind can carry itself only to a certain height within the world of divine spheres, no further.

The mystery schools have definite systems of discipline by which the whole nature of the individual can dissociate the elements of exoteric and esoteric knowledges through protracted effort to reach the level of supersensuous comprehension. Having reached this state, the principles of the higher knowledge are communicated to the neophyte by a method almost as arcane as the secrets themselves. This is a strange telepathic system developed so the findings of the subtler inner perceptions are communicated without passing through the place interval which exists between ordinary intellects – an interval which must be filled with words or other symbolic forms in which the esoteric matter is necessarily lost.

So the esoteric knowledge which man is trying to find is – the classification of those superessential elements of the pure intellect sphere where form, as man recognizes it, doesn't exist. Now you can see why such information cannot be found in books, lectures, and words or symbolic forms. This is why the reality scale has at top: Knowingness, Lookingness, Symbolism (as 3rd.). See? The esoteric knowledge must be communicated to the seeker by a method which, while it awakens no response in the sensory organisms, renders knowledge comprehensive to the inner perceptions. The subject of this inner knowledge and its method of communication has long confounded men of letters. Henri Bergson, French philosopher, has written extensively on the subject. His best work is: "The Creative Mind!" In other words science and religion can't conceive of the human mind functioning independent of matter; nor the possibility of mind thinking in terms independent of form. The similitudes of phenomena is independent of rational processes and the laws of comparison which dominate the field of material thought.

A postulate set by early mankind established that the physical universe will permit no energy to exist within its domain unless that energy abides by the dictates of matter by being clothed in the substances and form of matter. When thoughts abide in the mind they are thus launched into generation through words – which are their bodies – dimming, like the mortal vehicles, the lucidity of the inner nature. Words, like the Jivatma, function poorly in this gross world of generating spheres. Thus the law of generation. Thus words are exteriorized in trite and conventional forms.

Because of a lack of space and time, I cannot get enough down for you on this subject – but I will take up the individual parts of esoteric knowledge in the last twenty-five letters of this series!

One last word. While the mind is capable of receiving extrasensory perception it can't communicate these attenuated impulses and still preserve their integrity. Examples of this are: Havelock Ellis in his biography – also his "Dance of Life" – gives an example of the result of intense functioning in the reality of psychic idealism, which was so sensitized he couldn't write about it for twenty-five years, for fear of losing the feeling. Similar experiences are recorded in the lives of Meister Eckhart, Swedenborg, Dante Alighieri, Martin Luther, St. John of the Cross, St. Theresa, to name a few.

You can in time familiarize yourself with the Egyptian mysteries, Persian mysteries, Hindu mysteries, Greek mysteries, Cabirian mysteries of Samothrace, (the latter had a communication system in the initiation similar to our present radio wave system, and the Greeks used an electrical system much like ours today.)

You can get a lot of information from "Lectures on Ancient Philosophy," Manley Palmer Hall, and the books of Albert Pike.

More later.

Letters to Gail

May 20, 1963

Dear Gail:

You have read of the universes and other planes in The Tiger's Fang. I will attempt to elaborate somewhat on them in this letter, since you have asked pertinent questions several times.

The creation and order of the universe is unique and known only to those explorers of the spirit. The terminology "inner worlds" and "higher worlds" are the same, but often confuses readers, seekers of the spirit. The cosmogony of the Masters will be found quite different from those of all other systems. This is so because the Masters have a far greater range of knowledge than other men. Their field of operation lies far out and away from the physical suns and moons. They know about the creation and order of this universe of so many parts from personal study and exploration. They know the words of Jesus when he spoke as spirit: "Lo, my word will always be with you until this earth passes away into heaven." For someday the lower universe will be destroyed, and all Jivatmas will be put into a deep sleep and drawn into the higher world to sleep for a 1000 years or so until the lower world is either rebuilt or left destroyed for eternity. This is the thought behind Judgment Day in the Bible!

The entire universe of universes is divided into four grand divisions, each marked out and differentiated from the rest by certain characteristics. These four divisions are named: Pinda – the lower worlds including the physical which is composed of the coarsest matter, and where the vibration rate is lowest. This is the opposite end of the pole of the universes and therefore can be called the negative pole. It is divided into three divisions – Pinda being the lowest – and embraces the suns, stars, planets, moons, etc. Here the mortals live in semi-death, a condition of heavy inertia, etc.

Next, or just above the physical universe lies the second grand division called Anda, the lowest of the heavens. Its capital is called Sahasra-dal-Kanwal, meaning "thousand petalled lotus." Its name is taken from the great clusters of lights which constitutes the powerhouse of the physical universe, for out of that powerhouse flows the power that created and now sustains all worlds in the Pinda group. Each light has a shade of tint. Here live millions of people who were renowned people of all ages of history. Here is the great golden hall of divine wisdom where the Masters teach each evening, contacting Jivatmas from the Pinda world and pulling them into the astral, or Anda, for learning. I've studied there under Sudar Singh. You may study there but not be conscious of it. This is the first station on the upward path of ECKANKAR.

The next grand division is Brahmanda, meaning the egg of Brahm. This refers to its shape and also to the governor or Lord who is its ruler. This Brahm is supposed by most of the old rishis, or wise men, to be the supreme being of all creation, because they knew of no one higher. But the ECK Masters know that there is not only one Brahm, but countless numbers of Brahms, who are governors over so many planes within the Anda world, and the Brahmanda world; each plane circling about the supreme region in its own orbit, and each of them has its own governor or ruler. Brahm was the highest God known to the ancient wise men, or yogis, and so the name Brahm is retained to designate the ruler of the three worlds, including the physical universe. Jehovah, is the ruler of the first world, Pinda, according to the Jews. Brahm is supposed to be over all worlds below and this is why the words "Three Worlds" always occurs in all religious literature, Buddhist, Christian, etc.

The highest division is called Sat Desha. It is the region of truth and reality, and its name implies that, for Sat Desha means true country. It is the highest that one can go throughout the universes, although God dwells beyond this, and beyond God is another area, which I will take up later. This is the center of all universes, the capital of all the worlds, and from it flows all the powers of the Creator, into the worlds below; this is the home of the Creator, but not God. This is the country into which only the Masters may enter; however, they can carry any disciple they wish if he is considered worthy. This is the world beyond imagination—beyond the concepts of the human mind, and will be only that which one may know by being carried there by a Master.

From this center the great creative current flows outward and downward to create, govern and sustain all the regions below it. It passes out into the universe like a radio wave, pulsing toward the other worlds; it is the audible life current, coursing outward to make the worlds inhabitable. This region is that of immortality; it is the one which is unchangeable, perfect, deathless. It is divided into four divisions, each having a lord of its own, and each having characteristics of theirown, but slightly different. But overall is the great lord, the Lord of Light and Sound. There lords have many names, but they are mostly Indian, the highest being Anami Lok, second Agam Lok, third, Alakh Lok and last Sat Lok. Many religions have different names for them– but overall is the great lord often called Sat Nam, or Lord of Light. The place is so intense with light that it is impossible for mortal words to describe it.

These worlds are where one day you and I will go live. It is the place where all Jivatmas go–but unless they are free of the coarse karma they will not progress upward, and this is the reason one must be freed of the sanskaras. This will be fitted together like the pieces of a crossword puzzle as you reread the parts of letters covering karma, reincarnation. For as one drops his karma he goes upward into the other regions finally reaching the highest, and he never returns here. I will give you a letter soon explaining why the Jivatma leaves this highest region and makes his journey through the lower worlds.

Intellect will never take anyone to the higher region. Mind goes only to the second region and there is discarded as a thing of no further use. When the Jivatma enters into the highest region, Sat Desha, or true country, it is pure spirit, and it will find all its inhabitants are the same, in such countless numbers as no man can estimate, all enjoying the greatest conceivable happiness. This supreme world is quite unknown to any of the world religions, because their founders had never reached that exalted region. In substance and arrangement it is wholly unlike anything known in this world. It is so vast that if the entire physical universe, with its countless millions of stars, planets and suns were thrown into the sky of Sat Desha they would be entirely lost.

More later.

Letters to Gail

May 21, 1963

Dear Gail:

Sooner or later you will come across the word DHARMA, which is a word in the Indian religious systems. It appears often in other religions, and each will give it a different meaning. However DHARMA generally means the "Right Way, the Law of Life, that which ought to be done according to the true path." This is the Hindu version.

To Buddhists, according to the Mahayana school of esoteric Buddhism, the meaning is the ultimate reality. It comes from the word dhar, to uphold. It refers to the all-creative current, the Audible Life Stream, which not only creates all things, but sustains all things.

Sometimes the word is used for a look upon the face of a religious teacher, a master or holy man. The opportunity to see the master's countenance is prized in India by millions of those who are at the bottom of the social scale as a chance for enlightenment. The translation of the word Dharma is exactly equivalent to the word TAO. This latter word was the Chinese word for the WAY, and often as the Spirit, which again is the creative life force. Remember Jesus saying, "I am the Way!" Dharma is the Way in the Indian religions. The word was known in the old Persian religion Zoroastrianism, whose followers are today known as Parsees (there are not many left in this world), as ASA, and in the Vedic terminology as RITA. In the Moslem religion it is called ISLAM. In Christianity it is known as the WAY. But it is actually the all-creative force pouring down from the Sat Desha region. Dharma is the Way and its central theme is righteousness, a life in the complete harmony with the great law, meaning fundamentally in harmony with God, the SUGMAD.

Thus Dharma means righteousness and Adharma means unrighteousness, or the disobedience of the Law of Dharma. This brings us back into karma again for it is wrapped up with all forms of evil, as well as righteousness. Sin-Righteousness-Karma. These three cannot be separated. Both sin and righteousness create karma. In the sacred literature of India, Dharma righteousness is doing right, obeying the law, and this means doing "what is to be done." Adharma is disobedience of the Law of Dharma. The same teaching runs through all religions. The Law of Moses, the Eight-fold Path of Buddha, Will of

Allah-Moslem—in fact, the commandments of God, no matter by what name the system is called are all the same. What to do as written in the law, is regarded as righteousness—for it opens the channel so the creative force flows into the Jivatma, and this force is what the Jivatma lives, sustains itself upon, as the body does with meat and drink. Without it, the Jivatma draws inward upon itself and retires unto itself, and loses its ability to create (not loses, but forgets).

When one starts upon the spiritual path, he develops Danda (self-discipline) to serve the SUGMAD, and this helps him to establish Swadharma in his life. This word Swadharma means— "The law of one's own life, one's duty, self-imposed duties." This is important for the law of one's own life is when one starts the establishment of his own life of freedom, not until then, for man was made to have his own life within the worlds of the SUGMAD, depending only upon IT, instead of anything else. This gets pretty deep for it involves the Law of Manu. Manu was the great law giver to the Hindu race, as Moses was for the Jews. He divided the Indian race into four castes, about the same time Moses gave the Ten Commandments to the Jews.

All those entering into life on a spiritual path must be well-grounded in the fundamental laws of righteousness. He must practice real Dharma in his life for without it he cannot make the start, and this is the downfall of Christianity, who claim by ritual they can dissolve one of his past sins and baptise him into the church. The ECK Masters called this the Shariyat, the Law of Life, that which is to be done, or ought to be done.

Some other words which will be of use to you concerning Dharma are: First, DHARMA-MARG, meaning the way through the good works, or path of good works. In other words, certain schools of thought emphasize the path of Dharma as that which will lead into Samadhi (the form of deep meditation or trance state in which the meditator cannot distinguish himself from the object of meditation—hence, see the letter on Beingness again). This path is one mostly used by the Buddhists, Christians and most orthodox faiths. Secondly DHARMA-MEGHA, a kind of Samadhi, absorption of the mind into the object of meditation with complete detachment. Such a person is said to radiate a light like a mantle of glory. In this state the mind is freed from activity, inward or outward, through perfect detachment from the world of senses. It is a sort of perfect knowledge which comes from one who practices this state, and is claimed to be the end result of the path of Dharma, or Dharma-Marg.

This is a paradox for it is complicated, yet simple. The present religious systems today are not practicing Dharma as they should be. All historical religions, if examined, will show they consist of five basic elements. They are: (1) Superstitious assumptions; (2) Emotional extravaganzas; (3) Ritualistic ceremonies; (4) Metaphysical speculations; (5) Ethical principles. It all comes back to the point that religion is an individual experience—a realization! But it certainly is not an outward expression and cannot be couched in forms and ceremonies. Nor can it be bottled up in creeds like a can of vegetables, neither can it be given by one man to another nor written down in books. Thus the basic reason for the confusion which goes on in religious matters or systems is because every man's experience is different from another's—and today you will find that religion is no longer a religion but a sociological theory, none quite correct, yet from a point in which their own mocked-up Gods are creating miracles. But remember, if one puts enough considerations into an image, that image is given life and will return the postulates of the desires the worshipper puts into it. Example: If a statue is given enough considerations and postulates of that being an image of God, it will take on those considerations because the worshipper is blinded by maya, and believes in it. When it won't perform for him it is, he believes, because he has sinned and is not worthy of the gifts of his god. Hence, the miracles of the old gods, Jupiter, etc., as well as those in our churches today. Remember what Mary Austin said about her discovery that it was the principle behind the invisible veil which worked in prayer, and not the stone statue. Man invokes the principle thinking he is answered by the statue.

For a moment I got off the subject, but remember, Dharma is actually a part of the path, and not the whole path as some schools of thought try to tell us. But it is a necessary part of that path as you may soon learn.

More later.

Letters to Gail

May 22, 1963

Dear Gail:

The inner conflicts are many, in fact they are wrapped up in such deceptive packages that one might never know the answer to whatever is bothering him. Fear, I would say, is the largest conflict bothering people. At any age, period in history—fear is the basis of the whole picture bothering mankind.

Tensions are the cause of conflicts. The desire for something and the fear of not getting the object of the desire is normally the cause of most tensions. Social tensions are caused by society placing the individual under the controls called respectability and prestige. Respectability is overrated by a half-million times, because all it amounts up to is vanity and pride. So many times it is false pride. Now the desire for something outside one's self always sets up a tension within the individual. For example, if you should want a new dress and couldn't have it, a tension is established and society would call it a worthy ambition if you worked for enough money to get the dress; but if you stole the dress society would brand you an outlaw. Yet in the subconscious there would be no difference in how you got the dress, but the tension would be relieved when the dress came into your hands. On the other hand a third tension is set up when society brands you a thief because you haven't lived up to the laws set by man—that you shall not steal from one another. This sets a guilt pattern within the individual.

This, in a way, is how inner conflicts work. Let's take for example aggressiveness; it is a tension established by anger, because the objective mind (remember the letter on Depth Psychology?) is afraid of something gaining advantage over it. Anger is an outer form of fear, and expresses itself in those who are mostly considered inferior—the other is those who are quick to agree with their adversaries. Anger is always a protective device to cover up one's own weakness.

Tensions are common in man, both emotional tensions or mental tensions. And they are not without their benefit, for in setting up a tension, one forgets what may be actually bothering him. One metaphysical teacher I knew once said— if you set up a desire for something, don't keep the mind on it, for that will surely keep you from getting it, but establish another desire in the opposite direction or start a conflict which will take the mind off the original desire and it will start working for you, manifest itself without any obstacles which one creates when thinking about a desire.

The electro-magnetic field surrounding the body is subject to ridges, barriers and inflows. These inflows may come in a half-dozen ways: human communication, both verbal and silent, inflows from mechanical elements like noises, inflows from reading, inflows from the elements, weather, stars, planets, beings in outer space, beings in the spirit world, from the senses, etc. All these inflows may somehow form a ridge. For example, if you try to hold off something, a small ridge may start in the electro-magnetic field about you, and this can become an aberration, but if after established, the same type of incident recurs and nothing is done but your reaction to it, then a lock is established over the aberration and eventually a number of locks and the ridge becomes known as an engram. This engram can be established in past lives, and continue into this one. It can always be broken without much trouble. Now one of the ways you can measure or yardstick a person's problems is: The Dynamics of Life, or what you might call the Divisions of Life. They are Self, Sex, Group, Mankind: Life, which means the flowers, plants minerals, animals, insects, fish, etc.; MEST, meaning matter, energy, space and time, or the Earth materials which are inorganic; World of spirit or forces, and the Supreme Being.

The tensions, conflicts, or introversions of an individual's life can be on one dynamic, or all. For example, one can be introverted on Self, meaning that he is completely aberrated on Self, talks about himself, puts all attention on Self, lives only for himself. The Second Dynamic, Sex and Eighth Dynamic often go together, meaning that an individual may put the cause of his sex activities as the result of God's will, or he is afraid of sex activities because he will be punished by God. This is one of the places where the Catholic Church enters into the individual's life pointing out that sex is an activity which is personal, but encouraged by church in marriage to have children so the faith can have more followers. Opposite this is the factor the church frowns upon, condemns sex out of wedlock. Hence, the Second and Eighth Dynamic activities. At this moment I am somewhat stuck on the Fifth Dynamic because of my life with cats, etc.

These Dynamics are actually streams of spiritual forces playing across the life of the individual. When they are dammed, hindered or blocked, overstrained, or interfered with, trouble arises. As they inflow upon the individual passing through the electro-magnetic field around him ridges or barriers may be formed if hindered and out of them comes the engram.

Actually, the engram or the aberration is a picture filed away in the reactive bank (remember the letter on reactive bank, on images or pictures). They are electronic pictures, and to be rid of them one either explodes them or has somebody to explode them. These images are the cause of inner conflict in the individual. You may not even know what might be bothering the individual until the original picture is pulled out of his file cabinet and looked at – and this looking at will dissolve or explode the image. But as long as the picture is inside, in the file cabinet, ready to be pulled out and gazed at inside the head (by the watcher or Jivatma, who does the looking at the image) and reaction sets in by looking at the picture, there will always be tension or inner conflict when certain things arise; and so many times the individual may never know what is wrong.

So many individuals are aberrated on the Eighth Dynamic, for they allow their 'lives to be forced into narrow channels of religion, overbalancing until they become fanatics in this field. Religion will create powerful dictators, if allowed, and groups can have aberrations on the same thing. Example: the South, as a whole, is still stuck on the same track of the old caste system of ante-bellum days– an aberration of the Third Dynamic; communism is an aberration of the Fourth Dynamic for China, Russia and The Russian bloc.

I hope that this isn't confusing, but it's a matter of trying to show you how inner conflicts work. It is a part of Depth Psychology, and none of Freudian psychology, which is actually the Second Dynamic, Sex, for he based everything he knew on sex to create his system of psychology. Incidently, he was, it is said, an impotent man, who was afraid of wide spaces like streets, etc. None of this is hard to understand. . .

More later.

May 23, 1963

Dear Gail:

The subject is "The Tone Scale." This is a scale showing the survival performance from the lowest point of existence to the highest. This is a unique yardstick drawn up by Ron Hubbard a number of years ago, and is one of the best for determining where an individual stands on the existence scale of life.

Starting at the highest point which is 40, I will give you the barest outline of the scale and how it works. It is: 40 – Security of Beingness, or maybe serenity of beingness; 20 – is action; 8.0 is exhilaration; 4.0 – enthusiasm; 3.0 – conservation; 2.5 – boredom; 2.0 – antagonism; 1.8 – pain; 1.5 – anger; 1.1 – covert (hidden) hostility; 1.0 – fear; 0.9 – sympathy; 0.8 – propitiation (appeasement, sacrifice); 0.5 – grief; 0.05 – apathy; 0.0 – death; -1.0 – punishing bodies; -1.5 – controlling bodies; -2.2 – protecting bodies; -3.0 – owning bodies; -3.5 – approval from bodies; -4.0 – needing bodies; -8.0 – hiding.

Each segment on the scale is actually a band of emotional life. For example pain, anger, boredom, antagonism, etc., are all emotional bands in which one might get stuck. So many people you notice are stuck in the anger band, 1.5 on the tone scale. Many are stuck in appeasement or propitiation, which is 0.8 on the tone scale. Now if will take a real look at religion, that is Christianity, you will get an insight on it as a whole. It is at 0.8, propitiation, because people in it are trying appeasement from God, and the clergy are trying appeasement for the people. Newspapers, radio programs, TV programs, and magazines are generally at 1.5 anger on the scale, or 1.0 fear, or 0.9 sympathy. Preachers are generally at 1.0 fear, for they are always trying to sell the congregation to accept the Will of the Lord or suffer damnation.

So you see the tone scale can be used to measure the emotional side of the individual or a situation, or a group of people, a business firm, industry, news media, etc., and of course religions and churches. Look at some of the people you know and judge them; for example, your roommate, whom I would think (but not knowing of course) only from the physical expression, etc., that she would be in anger band, fear band and apathy band; moving from one to the other with frequency. A person can move up and down this scale in moments, days or weeks, but generally are stuck basically in one band. But you can begin to see after some study of the tone scale. And also you can start breaking up some of your own pattern of emotional habits after a time.

Now for a breakdown of the attitudes or bands.

40-27 Survival excellent; right in most things; takes full responsibility; owns all; good human relations; always cheerful; he is the motion source; speaks truth; good faith in self; knows; is cause, and I AM it-is serene.

27-22 I'll live forever; my actions are naturally right; I've full responsibility and act upon it; I may own it; but it's theirs, too; the future is endlessly beautiful; I can start and stop any motion at will; I can make any good thing real; I can trust on any dynamic and act accordingly; I know and use what I know; I can cause any good effects. I am myself. Exhilaration is the attitude here!

16.0-11.0 How could I do otherwise than live long? I'm glad that I'm in the right. I'll take responsibility; I wouldn't mind owning some things; I like my individuality; I can put so much into the future; I can straighten out what I don't trust; I understand; Causing action is wonderful; I am and they need me. The attitude is enthusiasm.

4.0-7.0 Courage and cheerfulness. I'm alive and like it. Things aren't serious. I enjoy possessions. The future holds so much.

2.0-4.0 Boredom and antagonism. Sometimes you don't survive. I guess we're all right, more or less right. Minor irresolution. You'd better be right. I don't mind responsibility. Maybe it's serious. You'd better take responsibility seriously. Possessions are often troublesome. I own in spite of them. I'm myself and I'll make the best of it. I've got to be myself somehow. The future can barely be faced. I adjust myself as needed. I can endure it. I'll stop if it threatens me and hurl it back. I like reality most of the time. Present reality can be endured. Reality is a threat. You can't trust things. I could understand if. . .If I find out I'll. . . You're not going to effect me. I'll be even if I don't like them.

1.0-2.0 Anger. Everything had better succumb but me. I'm right whenever I'm wrong. You're wrong. I'm afraid to be right. You're responsible. How serious things are. It's mine. I own people and destroy materials. I'm somebody. I hate whoever threatens me. The present is bad. I have to stop motion. I'll control people or die. All reality is perverted. I like gossip. I hate people. I'm too good for them. I only want to know enough to destroy. Obey me. I'll make an effect if it destroys me. I'm important.

0.5-1.0 Fear, cowardice, embarrassment, shame, grief. I guess I'd better succumb but maybe I'll take you with me. I can't survive it. I'm afraid to be right. I don't dare do anything wrong. Doubt. Indecision. I was wrong. If I had responsibility I'd be hurt. It's terribly serious. I was and I failed. I'm afraid I'll lose. I have to hide it. I've lost. Maybe I'm not even myself. I'd better be another, I'm too painful, there is no future or present. The past is all there. Waiting for something to show up. Motion goes through me. It is better not to be real. Lies are best. I've lost my illusions, reality is so painful. Life is threatening. I'll betray you. I'm betrayed. I'm trying not to know, but. . .Gullible, credulous about fearful things. Life has effected me terribly. Cause may effect me permanently. Life has affected me terribly. I would be myself if others would let me.

0.0-0.5 Apathy. I'm waiting to succumb. Everything is beyond right and wrong. All is wrong. I'm not even responsible for myself. I'd better not own anything. I'm nobody. I can't face the past. I'm powerless before any motion. Things are never real. I don't know anything. I'm lost. I'm a nobody.

0.0 Dead. Wrong. No responsibility. Owns nothing. Nobody. Never will be anything. Stopped for all motions. Has hullucinations. I know not anything. I have full effect. I am not anything, only a rock or a log. Anything can out create me.

These are expressions and attitudes which you will find in the emotional bands of the individual, groups, and nations. Afterwhile you can start having insight into the nature of a person by study of the tone scale, by reading the newspaper or a magazine article about the man. You can find out about the president through his yardstick, by measuring his statements, his actions and deeds, through newspapers, magazines and TV appearances.

More later.

Letters to Gail

May 24, 1963

Dear Gail:

The subject is "Hypnotism." Since hypnotism is done on a mental level you must get the point that there is nothing spiritual in the subject or partaking of it. It is one of the lower forms of occultism used many times by a magician to make known his wishes to the followers and get them on the right path for whatever he desires of them. Hypnotism can be said to be the drawing of a person's attention to such a concentrated point that he leaves his subjective mind open to suggestions through commands from an outside source. There really isn't much to the practice, once a person can get its knack, for following out the definition I've just given you it's easy to say that one in love is hypnotized.

Our society has all men, that is most of them, hypnotized. The characteristic of the society is generally recognized. What is less often recognized is that this society, like all others, is more than simply an expression of the relationship of man to nature; it also exemplifies a particular relationship of man to man: namely, some men's dominance over other men. All our institutions express the way in which one group of men dedicated to certain ends imposes its dominance over other men. Our society is above all the expression of the dominance that the large scale capitalist exerts over all other persons. What makes our modern society something new in history is the new ways that these concentrated economic, political and military elites have of imposing social dominance over the individual. The paradox is this: so great is the power that society can exert against the individual that it even subjects to dominance those very elites who seem to rule. At this stage of our industrial civilization, rule becomes even more impersonal, something outside the grip of any individual. This new society and its shaping of our lives presents to us, in a particularly pressing way, the need for a new moral philosophy. We cannot be independent of the forces that make our mass culture far too profound simply to make that change, nor is the individual any longer in control to make changes.

This is the point where hypnotism come in. We are hypnotized by our ability to produce and consume on a national scale. If we are that gullible, as a society, then the individual is subjected to the danger of mass hypnotism. Hypnotism can be dangerous. Not long ago an amateur hypnotist in Denmark was sentenced to life imprisonment for inducing a hypnotic subject to kill. Given the right combination of hypnotist and subject, hypnosis can be a lethal weapon. Didn't Hitler hypnotize his people into subjection and unleash war on the world? Sensible people can, however, be victimized by the more subtle techniques of hypnosis, as indeed they are every time they fall for advertisements that extol their virtues rather than the virtues of the products concerned, and every time they vote for political candidates who run on platforms of flattery or fear. Hypnosis in disguise is far more dangerous than hypnosis in the open.

Hypnosis has to do with the subconscious mind. In the field of medicine it has been applied mostly to neurology. It has achieved both prestige and fame in the field as an investigative and curative tool. Many early medical pioneers in France worked on nervous disorders with hypnosis. Dr. James Braid, a Scot, put his patients in trance for curative measures of rheumatism, headaches, epilepsy and strabismus (crosseyes). His findings were rejected by the British Medical Society. It wasn't until 1958 that the Medical Society adopted it as an arm of medicine. Hypnosis is a state of the body as well as the mind, and this is why it is important to everyone. All the body changes hypnosis can create are brought about by psychological rather than physical means. Because hypnosis can be induced so easily and because anyone can become a hypnotist, hypnosis, in the wrong hands, can lead to dangerous consequences. Under hypnotic state the spontaneous eruptions of the subconscious can be good—from its eruption in genius and creativity to its eruption in psychopathology—in automatic writing, automatic speech, multiple personality, phobias, compulsions, hallucinations, and delusions. Any control exerted over the appearance of these phenomena is done by the person to whom they occur.

The hypnotic subject experiences the hypnotist's will as his, to do things he could not do with his normal waking life. This new will is more powerful than his own in his waking life. It depends upon the degree or depth of the hypnotic trance how strongly the hypnotist's will can be forced upon the subject. One out of every five persons can be hypnotized to the depth of somnambulism, in which awakened he retains no memory of the events of his trance. He becomes the operator, who uses the ears, eyes, and other senses for himself. The bizarre classical phenomena of hypnosis is associated with this sleep-waking state. It is in this state the subject is enabled to do things far beyond his power of voluntary action in normal life. The person in deep trance will appear asleep unless the operator has him act as if awake, and can simulate normal consciousness so well it is almost impossible to detect his actual state. He can develop all sorts of hallucinations like eating raw onions, and tears coming to his eyes, etc.

In this deep trance the person can be made oblivious to pain; he can undergo major surgery (Ghandi did this once, by self-hypnosis) without anesthetic. The hypnotist can take over control of the functioning of each organ in the subject's body, making his heart rate go up, raising or lowering his body temperature, and changing his subject's basal metabolism. He can be regressed back into childhood, or other lives, or progressed into his future lives, or ages. He can be given post-hypnotic commands to carry out. There was a case or two during World War II, in which the Americans hypnotized a soldier and sent him into the Nazi army ranks to find out their military plans. Acting as a spy he had been given orders to forget everything until his return. And upon his return, the code word was given which unlocked the secrets he learned, and then he was de-hypnotized. This has been an old trick among the orientals in the past. Many have learned foreign language under hypnotism, and given the post-hypnotic suggestions that it would be retained.

There are also ways of self-hypnosis, through suggestions to the subconscious, mostly done by standing in front of a mirror at specific times and telling one's self what is expected, or ordering certain things for the body or mind to carry out. I think it's Ingelness who tells in his book about hypnosis done by telepathy; this isn't hard either, for anyone who tries to portray an open mind is more open to hypnotic suggestions through telepathy–this society is teaching its people toleration, which means to be opened-minded about relationships with each other. This is a little crazy, for open-minded means the ability of a subtle hypnotic operator made easier for control of another person's mind. He can control this mind by subtle devices—fear, anger, unhappiness, glittering promises, etc. He can even put the subject into a hypnotic trance by use of clever tricks which the subject never knows.

A good book to read on the subject is Hypnotism by G. H. Estabrooks. By the way, when you want to impress anyone speak to a point behind his head; let the vibrations of your voice flow around him to that point; in giving orders or anything else.

More later.

Tal

Letters to Gail

May 25, 1963

Dear Gail:

The subject is: "Other Worlds and Civilizations." Much of the phenomena we are getting today such as flying saucers, telepathy from other planets, strange sights in the heavens and stories of visitors from other planets is not all completely fiction, although one has to be somewhat rational in order to keep his feet on the ground and not let his imagination run away from him, nor be so gullible that every story is one to believe. It takes a bit of experiencing and testing to see what might be somewhat truthful, although much has never been explained, and probably will not! Within this universe are over a thousand stars and planets of size that could possibly contain life. Most of the major planets are liveable according to scientists and astronomers. So far ninety-odd galaxies have been counted which means world systems according to our own, exist.

The only way to know and understand the other worlds is through exteriorization (leaving the body in the Jivatma form) and exploring it yourself. But do this only with someone who knows the areas or something may happen. Again, I am not speaking of the spirit worlds, but the physical worlds which exist elsewhere in this universe. Take for example, most of the way stations are on the other planets; meaning that stations have been established for those traveling to and fro between the physical worlds. In my book, Talons of Time, I describe a wide number of these stations. There is station No. 9 on the far side of the moon, where those moving back and forth to the Earth will make their stops. The lack of oxygen there won't allow physical bodies, but those in astral or Jivatma forms. One makes a step fifteen feet there because of lack of gravity, hence in this station the steps are 15-20 feet, while here on Earth, 6 inches or so.

The planet of Mars is fully inhabited according to those who have been there. The civilization is rather monolithic in structure, with several types of races, from the dwarf race to the majestic beings who have large and superior mental powers. The landscape is rather weird; vivid colors, strange plants, a sky which is high yellow, mountains and earth a sharp red color, and an architecture of buildings which is rather oriental in style, but not completely, maybe it would look more gothic mixed with oriental styles. Most of the people wear togas or robes, some breech cloths, but the peasants have only sacks thrown over their bodies to cover nakedness. The climate is hot, dry and acrid. Bodies are fleshy.

Jupiter, Venus, Clarion, and Pluto are inhabited by Jivatmas which are completely without physical bodies. They live in worlds similar to the world of Tibet, high terrain, smoky seas and vast distances. They each speak a different language, and can communicate with each other, like one nation on Earth communicates with the others through some common language—but it is mostly on thought level. Now these planets are generally higher developed in the races, but individuals are similar to what might be here. We have the wise, the thinkers and the highly intelligent, along with the ignorant—these planets have the same. Much of my experience in contacts with other worlds has not proved to me that they have greater superior intellect as a civilization, although their mechanical devices are better, sciences are greater and their form of education is solely different. But their forms of government have not been developed above the monarchy type of government, that is a benevolent ruler subject to the council of so-many advisors or a parliament. Their social life is completely different from our lives because they are more creative, and have forms of entertainment more along the theatre than we have—nothing hardly can be found here that would be like this earth's form of entertainment in athletics and social activities. They go in for heavier type of mental and aesthetics than we.

Now Mercury, Uranus and Saturn are the enemy planets in a sense. They are supposedly inhabited by those races who are always trying to gain territories. They are completely warlike—and by the way Mars does belong in this group. According to ancient history, what I learned in India, there have been five invader waves to this Earth planet from outer space. That is why the Aryan race is supposedly the great race of this Earth—because they were the founders of the original colony upon this Earth coming here from Jupiter. Later a few other colonies were settled here from Venus and Clarion. The reason for these colonies was to establish a claim to this Earth planet before the warlike tribes from the other planets could get here. There have been wars over the Earth planet as well as other planets within this orbit. While thinking about it, the center of this universe has its place in the milky way, and it is supposedly from this center all the ruling power comes forth to all planets. The Aryan people took flesh bodies, and have found ways of protection against the other races. The colonies founded by Saturn and the war planets were supposedly the dark-skinned people who settled in the hot countries, because the climate was similar to that of their own world.

Now when a Jivatma leaves the body at death it doesn't necessarily go off to the astral world or the invisible worlds. It can be trapped and sent off to the mother planet where it will be used like a Zombie. This is what might be called a Jivatma trap—which is a most interesting subject to anyone, especially to an invader from outer space. You trap a Jivatma by curiosity, by giving him awards and prizes, or an implant, by retractor screens, by mock-ups, by ornate buildings which he will enter unsuspectingly only to be trapped, and it is by such means that a Jivatma is reduced from knowing to a colonist, a slave, a MEST (flesh) body.

All Jivatma traps have one thing in common; they use electronic force to lure the Jivatma into forgetting, into unknowingness, into effect. Their purpose is to rid the area of those nuisances, the Jivatmas who cannot be policed, and to gain personnel for their own slavery work.

Now for a few explanations. An implant is—to introvert the Jivatma, make him look at himself, think he is guilty of something, that something is wrong with him. A retractor screen is—a screen set in front of the Jivatma to make him look at himself and see how bad he is. Now hold on to your hat—for this statement is not going to set well—for I'm moving you completely into another thought area. Mysticism is a Jivatma trap—it glues the Jivatma (Soul) to the MEST body, and those who have the name of being great mystics were not so spiritually developed as their admirers' claim for them. When reading their works it is easy to tell just how far they got in their lives up the ladder of spirituality. It is a strange thing but not many people know the foundation of the philosophy which I'm trying to get across to you. I want to go into this deeper in another letter.

More later.

Letters to Gail

May 26, 1963

Dear Gail:

The subject is "Jivatma Psychology" (meaning Soul or spiritual psychology). This universe, despite the talk of the religionists, is one of survival, and only the strong can survive it, only the ruthless can own it. If you are spiritually strong you can survive it, and do not wish to own it, but if you are ruthless you can own it, but cannot survive it. Given a weak spot, a being cannot long endure it for this universe will seek it out and enlarge it.

Fighting this battle for survival, and fight it man must, a being in a MEST (Matter, Energy, Space and Time) universe cannot seem to afford decency or charity or ethics; he cannot afford any weakness, and mercy. The moment he does this he is lost—for he is surrounded by all those forces wishing to destroy him which no matter the state of aberration of his social surroundings, will engulf him instantly if he ceases to obey the very least laws of MEST. So you see, this is a universe of force. It is not a universe of reason. Brutal, unthinking, without decency or mercy, MEST forces await the punishment of any being with any weakness. This is why all philosophies, all social systems, all religions have failed. None have taken into account that this is a dangerous universe and that the flesh of man is always under attack from bacteria, and many invisible microbes which feed on the flesh on the MEST body.

Therefore, the possession of a MEST body is a liability, for through that body the being can be given pain, can be regimented by the routine demands of eating and care from harm until, at the very highest, he can be but a puppet dancing to the spin of some unthinking planet under the strong glare of a remote and careless sun. Under these conditions a being, burdened with the care and liability of a body made uncertain by an unknowingness, bows to strange and nonexistent gods, resorts to terrible make-shifts in lieu of justice, cringes before the H-bomb, and the weapons of destruction, law, war and MEST.

So you soon learn that the philosophers and religions have this to say: "Only can you defeat life through dying." Christianity, Buddhism, and most of the oriental religions have been saying this for centuries. But none have come up with the answer as yet. Our cult today is called

"Worship the body." Medical doctors, school teachers, parents, traffic officers, the whole society unite in the war cry, "Care of the body." Even many religions will shout this war cry. This stems from the ignorance that the latter has not been successful in their own teachings – that we are the Jivatma and that is all there is to our own being.

Alone, the body can live, talk, react, sleep, kill and direct an existence no better than that of a zombie. Put a Jivatma in charge of it and it becomes possessed of ethics, morals, direction and goals and the ability to reason. It has a total devotion to avoid pain, seek survival factors and beget new bodies. It is a carbon-oxygen machine which runs at 98.6 F. The Genetic Entity runs this machine, but under the direction of a Jivatma it has better survival patterns.

Now compared with the MEST the Jivatma is the controlling factor in the universe if in good tone condition, otherwise It is an effect. It is capable of creating the electronic flow, meaning an electrical flow. It is also capable of producing considerable voltage and amperage, enough to give somebody a very bad shock, to put out his eyes or cut him in half. The Jivatma on Its own can instill anything on the emotional range into another being for each emotion is a wave length and wave characteristic.

A Jivatma can be rendered unconscious by wave action; it can be hypnotized; it can be made to sleep; it can be made to possess facsimiles and use them. It can be aberrated in such a fashion as to forget Its identity. It is subject to all the laws and rules of thought, emotion and effort, and it has enormous choice in their use. A Jivatma can be de-aberrated by ridding It of Its chains of facsimiles and restoring It to Its knowledge-identity. A Jivatma can enjoy existence and emotional impact. It can plan and act. Its activities are very high on the tone scale. It is very high aesthetically and devotes most of Itself and time to aesthetics. It has a high sense of justice.

A Jivatma can be made visible by certain electronic flows; It can be pinned down by certain flows. It motivates MEST bodies–but the GE tries to trap the Jivatma and harass It and use It to motivate new bodies. Jivatma will attack other Jivatmas who menace It. It can kill MEST bodies by throwing charges at them. They quarrel with one another by showing each other facsimiles (pictures) or throwing energy flows at one another, but they are not quarrelsome. It communicates with other Jivatmas by telepathy. It can move at high speed, It is not bound by atmosphere or temperatures, It can move material objects by throwing an energy flow at them. It can pass out in the form of a solid, apathetic slumber and stay in it until It is awakened by another Jivatma or a Master. It can feel pain. It can be crippled and dismembered but it requires a force which would blow half a town off the map, and It will regrow the parts again like a crawfish will a new limb. It can read books a couple of countries away—like London—from Its position in New York City.

A Jivatma likes to collect facsimiles like a postal stamp collector. Sometimes It even purloins packages of facsimiles from other Jivatmas. Thus It has a record of Its own experience, of the things which actually happened to It, and a whole bank of "seconds" or second facsimiles or photographs It has taken from other Jivatma banks. It lives Its life in segments: the largest segment is composed of spirals; as It goes through the MEST universe, It is involved in a series of spirals each one less in terms of years, ordinarily, than the last. The first spiral which occurred 70 or 74 trillion years ago, might have been as long as a trillion years, but the next spiral after that was a little shorter. Succeeding spirals have been shortened. The present spiral for most is about 40,000 years long, although some are on a longer spiral than this. A spiral can be subdivided into lives, such as the current one which is only one division of the current spiral.

None of this is complicated. Now there is a term called Obsession. This is an incident in which the Jivatma has a feeling that It must have a certain amount of pictures in order to know. This is a control trick used by other Jivatmas on It, to make It think It must have a set of pictures; this aberrates It and makes It easy to handle. The educational systems of our civilization are fine examples of where Jivatmas get their facsimiles without feeling that they steal them.

Jivatmas sometimes trap MEST bodies, and run them like work animals, for the fun. They can also run two bodies in the same place, one in a trance and the other actively. Often done, but it is not a good policy for it gets the operator mixed up sometimes.

More later.

Paul

Letters to Gail

May 27, 1963

Dear Gail:

The subject is "Jivatma Traps." The Jivatma may be trapped by emotional pain, sex, mysticism, surgery, facsimiles, mockups, physical, if it has a MEST body, desire for physical possessions, body worship, borrowing pictures, and a half-dozen or more other things you see around you daily, including loyalty, faith, and the qualities used by any orthodox religion.

Now some of the ways a Jivatma may trap other Jivatmas is through the retractor waves. That is to say that one Jivatma can send out a wave length which will act as a retractor force with something else. This beam is sometimes called a tractor beam which means that the Jivatma can pull the object right up to itself. Therefore it is very easy to batter the Jivatma into unconsciousness and pull it up against a wall like a fly; to trap it there for as long as the aggressor desires. Sounds a little strange, but anyone with absolute self-possession can work out a lot of ways to trap a Jivatma even after it has become what might appear to be a physical captive of a group. Remember this, the more the force of an individual is cancelled out by counter-forces, the lower he gets on the scale of attitudes. Hit by strong forces, the Jivatma begins to conceive that it isn't anything, that it is a nothing—and when it gets to this point it disbelieves.

Invalidation by force is the answer to much of our crime today. Invalidation of the individual makes him become so degraded by force invalidation that he devotes himself to the vegetable thing called a body in a last ditch effort to control some part of the environment. He is invalidated to a nothingness, so the body has to become something. Therefore, he is trapped; for example, the racial question in the South amounts up to the whites being invalidated by the coloreds, on one hand, and on the other invalidated by the government so they become as an individual group a nothingness, and after a while, in order to counter-act this, take up a fight against those forces which made them invalidated. This force could lead to a full scale, but minor war against either side. The invalidation scale runs like this: (1) Criticism and Counter-Criticism are the overt and motivator invalidations on the thought level. (2) Misemotionalism and Counter-Misemotionalism are the overt and motivator invalidations on the emotion level. (3) Physical force and Counter-Physical force are the overt and motivator invalidations on the effort level.

Thought, emotion and effort can hang up one on the time track, and keep him trapped in such a way that he will be a willing or unwilling, but at least an obedient, slave or to get him out of the area and keep him from running away thereafter or to nail him into complete useless immobility. The society wants him to have a good reaction to police threats (and most psychotics will become more psychotic immediately after a police interview, no matter how innocent it was). He is required to leave the MEST body alone and respect it. Furthermore, the now trapped Jivatma will turn on its fellow-Jivatmas who are free and any that it didn't like; it wants to start running and keep running or, barring that, to be immobile MEST thereafter.

Another way of trapping a Jivatma is to give it a box of pictures, and since it is disposed of collecting pictures it will get so absorbed in them, that it will spend years looking at them like a child does in a picture-book. This is partly from curiosity, and partly from interest. You will find this type Jivatma (when in a MEST body) to be very curious about cereal boxes which have pictures inside them. A Jivatma which is high on the tone scale can pick up and discard pictures at will. Almost every Jivatma has a fear of losing its facsimiles, and the collapse of its time track.

Sometimes an implant will trap a Jivatma. If it is given a strong postulate by another Jivatma, it might follow out that postulate to a completeness. For example, this is an exaggeration but makes for a picture of what can happen. If an implant is given a Jivatma—say a strong forgetter implant, shot into him and then he is told that he is a rock and will sit on the side of a mountain for ten thousand years, it's done, until one day another Jivatma comes by and sees him. "What are you doing there, Charley?" The implanted Jivatma says, "I'm a rock, you fool. Anybody can see that!" Of course, the passing Jivatma gives him the word that he's really not a rock but a Jivatma, breaking the spell. This is so often done among Jivatmas. Remember so many keep constantly telling a child that he is stupid and after a while he believes that. Same idea—but on a higher scale and the Jivatma is hypnotized into believing he is a rock and will try to act like one.

The zombies of the Haiti Voodoo legend were bodies without the

Jivatma inside them. They are driven out by some Jivatma who has a terrible knowledge of what he can do with black magic, and uses the bodies for slave labor. The Jivatmas which have been driven out of the body are trapped and held somewhere, maybe put to sleep, or driven up against a wall and held there by electronic beams so they cannot escape. This all sounds wild but it is true—I'm aware that it's getting ahead somewhat for you—but if you don't try to think hard it will all start working out in your mind faster.

Much of the devices used for traps to keep the Jivatma caught are of a hypnotic, stimulus-response variety. One of the best examples of this today is the university education which makes a filecard system out of the mind for the supposed thinking individual. The use of the subconscious as taught now by most so-called mystics and occult leaders is simply a Jivatma trap and many cults like the Aquarian Foundation are a trap for their followers. I don't mean to say that everything is a trap but most traps are simple, so simple that you can catch them first handed—and they go like this: "You're guilty so you must pay the penalty or let my church, my group or myself rid you of that guilt!" Most groups will want to set up a guilt pattern in the individual to make him look at himself and tell himself what a bad fellow he is—and that he is awful! Even wives will do this to husbands, or vice versa. Most cults use this device! Most churches, religions use it also, like implanting one with the original sin idea! When anyone sets out to invalidate you or degrade you, look out! He may be trying to set you a trap; or when anyone tries to arouse your curiosity to the point you are going to investigate—then beware—this might be a trick which he is setting up. Remember advertising? The old curiosity hook is used here to make a person want to look at the merchandise and slammo he's sold. (Remember the article on Yang and Yin.) Same principle!

Here is an interesting thing. Know how many types of psychology there are? Seventeen, or more. They are: Applied, Industrial, Social, Practical, Corporation, Education, Pathological, Religious, Structural, Physiological, Purposive, Animal, Child, Ethnopsychology, Genetic, Psychotherapy, Psychical, to name a few. These are broken down into subdivisons. See how long it takes to learn one branch of psychology. Don't think you can get spiritual psychology in a few letters.

More later.

Paul

May 28, 1963

Dear Gail:

One must be strong to be able to survive the study and readings, meditations, thinking and seeking in the spiritual field. It is the emotionally and mentally unstable who seek philosophic writings. I have seen many minds disintegrate apparently under the influence of Kant, Spinoza, Nietzsche, Buddhism, Biblical, etc., not to mention the exponents of occultism, mysticism and new thought.

There is a reason behind all this. That reason being that the average person doesn't have the strength to understand what he is studying, and too many times he becomes too far overbalanced, stretches out too far and loses himself in the darkness of the mind. One of the characters in "Kings' Row," by Henry Bellamann, goes insane because she has moved too far out in her mind and cannot get back to what is called solid ground. The illogic of the life beyond the material life is too much for some minds, and they cannot under any circumstances be logical again, and this is what makes friends, relatives and kin believe in their craziness, and will often seek to lock them behind bars.

The real truth which many thinking people are coming to see is the legal and moral repression of normal instincts is disastrous. The ECK Masters have long been aware that the damming up of human emotions is not only ineffective but produces other evils in its train that are worse than the original fault. The problem, of course, lies farther back than any mere censorship or law against some adult action, whether it be in moral or civil action. Wise men know that the real work can be done in the harming of the youth today, and in that field, despite the revolution that has taken place in the intellectual and spiritual world about us, we are still ignoring the great problem that has shamed mankind throughout the centuries by its age-long neglect: the failure to tell the truth to the masses of people; the truth of spiritual reality, and not the drummed up false theory given by a set of priests or lawmakers to keep the people in control. Out of that hypocrisy grows most of our modern evils of moral and spiritual censorship. And that deserves discussion here.

Now the whole truth that when man dies he goes into a lighter body for the next world is not being taught to people. Some jazzed up theory about a purgatory and a hell has long gone out of style but it leaves a complete void by which the people are not interested in learning. For example, most people live in hope of getting something better. When one dies, he is generally met by a relative, friend or a guide who will take care of him until he can be placed properly in another environment similar to his own. He takes up where he left off on earth, but something strange will take place, and that is the vocabulary – which is mostly by mental telepathy. The nouns over there are literal – meaning if one talks about water, he means water and not used as a slang. He talks about goats, he doesn't mean something human, but actually that animal which is a goat. He must learn to not think any further in the vernacular as on earth.

Life on the other side is pleasant. The body, which the Jivatma has taken to meet with the vibrations of that plane, is youthful, light and generally more handsome than the earth body. The individual finds that life there is much as what goes on here except that people are more creative, and they are friendlier and work for one another, in a different manner than this earthy way. Sympathy has no place in the afterworlds; there is a feeling of well being, a desire to do something if one needs a helping hand, and many do, but the individual gives his aid because he understands–not for the purpose of sympathy. Sooner or later you will find sympathy is a trap–it was a great trap that Abe Lincoln fell into and finally it caused him unusual sorrow, and this sorrow brought sorrow to a whole nation, and almost split it in half, and we are still experiencing today the result of his sympathy. This has nothing to do with racial questions, but to do with entanglement in which the emotional feelings will get, and trap the individual, this is a part of the Jivatma traps. If you watch people who have great sympathy for others, you will note that they are in a trap for they cannot control their sympathy, and it generally gives them trouble somehow. I am not saying that one shouldn't have sympathy, or any of the emotions, but one should learn to control these emotional states, so as to give his feelings in the right directions; on the other hand he cannot afford to go overboard in coldness of emotions either.

There are also great wars which go on in the astral world between forces which are trying to gain control over the others. One of the great principles of occultism is "As above so below, and so below as above." In other words what we do here emotionally reflects above and vice versa. So if there is a war going on in heaven it will reflect here on earth and the reverse is also true. This is why in many cases when a great battle is going on, as in World War I, or in World War II, that a battle was seen in the sky, between two great forces; this is why many battles going on in heaven are reflected on earth in both image and reality. Whatever is happening in heaven generally happens on earth. In other words earth is the reflecting image of the heavens.

Earth is a trap for the Jivatma, and when the body dies it means the Jivatma, if it realizes its own self-control (or by being cause) and has the knowledge, as I'm trying to show you, then it can go right ahead in the other world with a guide showing it around; and after that it is far ahead of the others. It doesn't have to depend upon anyone much, except to get its bearings, as you would if you went to a foreign country. You'd have to get some landmarks so you could learn to get about yourself. That is about it, except that you must pass the Angel of Death, and this is easily done if you have the knowledge and are familiar with the procedure before reaching his gate. The Angel of Death is that official who decides whether you should go back to earth for another incarnation, or can pass through the gates into Paradise. We jokingly call this entity St. Peter, but it isn't true, for St. Peter has a far greater task than this—and besides he is above the astral world doing some duty for the Catholic heavenly officials. If you know enough about death, its procedures and the Angel of Death, you can take any Jivatma across the borders of death into heaven. I know several individuals who are doing this today as a part of their duty to the higher command. I will tell you about them one of these days if you like.

This is why I said in the beginning that some disintegrate under the study of occultism, mysticism and new thought. One has to have a certain amount of training and knowledge before starting along the path. It is the same as formal training. No one can expect to start in at the college level without the foundation of a grammar school and high school education. It wouldn't make sense—and that is the reason I've taken so much trouble to get knowledge across to you emphasizing practically two things: being discreet in your manner with whom you talk, of what to read, and people and events. These must be adhered to without failure, or suffer!

More later.

Letters to Gail

May 29, 1963

Dear Gail:

The subject is "The Spiritual Hierarchy." This will seem very complicated because the various occult and religious groups have their own names for the ladder of Gods. Actually we are pantheistic (many gods) in nature, rather than a single God whose worship is called monism, which is the way of the orthodox religions since the time of the Jewish influence on the world, yet the eastern religions had a system of monism mixed with pantheistic worship.

At the lowest scale of the ladder are the four elements. The earth creatures, called gnomes, *which are in charge of the earth elements, gold, silver, other minerals, etc.; the fairy tales are alive with them; next are the* salamanders, *the fire elementals, which live in the fire and look like small lizards or dragons and they take care of the fire; sometimes destructive, sometimes for the good of man; next are the* undines, *which are the water spirits, which live in the world of water and take care of that element for the higher beings. Then fourth are the* sylphs, *which are the air spirits, known in fables as fairies. They control the air elements, and are gentle until they are disturbed or become angry and the storm is the result of their rages. They look like graceful, young women. The undines are the mermaids which legend has given us. But the elementals were used by the magicians for their own purposes.*

The next step is the planetary spirits who send the forces of spiritual power toward the earth. These are under the one great spirit, known as Jehovah, who rules this world, and under him is the legion of angels who conducts his affairs. Many believe that Jehovah, or Yaweh, is God. The masters of the earth are responsible to this deity unless they have developed beyond him, toward God himself.

Each planet, star, etc., in these universes have their own hierarchy as I've just named. However, you go past these to the astral world where there is a similar set of Gods, under a ruler called Niranjan, who also rules the earth and all the worlds of matter. This god has a set of angels at his bidding and works strongly in the psychic field. Each world as you travel upward has a god, or great spirit in charge, for example: Kal Niranjan, (just named); Omkar, Ramkar, Sohang, Sat Nam, and the Sat Purusha (called God) the nameless one. Within these five planes or seven planes rather, are the numerous planes which each have their own rulers and hierarchy of the spirit. These are the four grand divisions and their rulers including the highest in which dwells the Absolute. The first three are called the three worlds which you read so much about in occult literature. They are ruled over by Brahm, (according to the Hindus) but other religions have a different name for him – they think that this is the highest world.

Since all worlds within these three worlds are under the Brahm or Lord as the Christian religions call Him, they see that he is a creator, but a weak God who has to put up a constant fight with the so-called devil. This is true for on the opposite end of the spiritual pole is Kal Niranjan, the completely negative God; who is always attacking the upper God to gain the kingdom of the world. The real contestant in the upper area is one God named Maha Kal who is often mistaken for Brahm, and known to the earthlings as Christ the Lord, or Buddhi, or any other name in religion meaning God. Many believe that by pushing past him to Brahm is actually finding the true God of all creation. Not true.

These ruler spirits exist in each religion but they have different names and you will find that they are worshipped the same but under various titles. The Mohammeds call God, Allah, Indian worshipers often give him the Akshar, Purusha, and in Indian literature was the ancient name Varuna, Zoroaster called him Ormuzd, and the Norsemen had the name of Thor for him. The American Indians spoke of him as Manitou. Most saints call him Anami, the nameless one.

The first manifested individualization of the Absolute is Agam Purusha, who is the lord of the lowest region in Sat Desha, the fourth grand division. Each individual member of this grand hierarchy is Lord God over all below him, and through each one of them all power flows to below him. Upon each planet also there are many subordinates working under the orders of the planetary ruler. At the foot of this grand hierarchy stands the entire human race; and among all the men of the world are vast numbers of individuals who are selected by the planetary ruler to perform certain functions and duties. As a rule, they are not aware that they have been so selected and empowered. Nevertheless, they are working under orders, whether they know it or not, and they must serve the Supreme Power, whether they will or not.

The masters occupy a unique place in this grand hierarchy. They do not work under the orders of any planetary ruler, or subordinate of the grand hierarchy, but under the orders of the Absolute Himself. They are his chief executives on earth, and they have a special duty, different from that of all others of the hierarchy, that is to take the Jivatmas out of the maelstrom of the material worlds, and take them up to the supreme region where liberty will be found. They have this unique service assigned to them, because there is no other way that the Jivatma can escape from this bondage, this house or prison, unless he stumbles upon the secret of the deliverance by accident, and takes himself upward.

The saint is the only being who has the power to come and go throughout the universe at will. He can travel in any land without hindrance where the others must be subjected to the laws of the universe in which they are in at that particular time. This is why the wise student of the spiritual worlds will get close to a saint, if possible, for he will carry them anywhere in the divisions possible.

Now within the negative stream in the lower worlds, under Kal Niranjan, is the famous trinity so named by the Hindu and catholic religionists. The laws of nature are actually the laws of this negative power, and all those morals and ethics we build up come out of this power. The system whether we like it or not is one which we can call a dictatorial one, for we must accept it or keep pushing around the bottom of the bucket until we do. So far as I know, at the present, there isn't anything else for the welfare of man in the spiritual world. If so I haven't found it.

The spiritual hierarchy isn't complicated, but it is a long drawn out process of study if one undertakes to make a detailed study. I really don't know any books on the subject; perhaps "The Secret Doctrine," by Madam Blavatsky, the Theosophyist. It has so much in it that I can't hazard a guess at times what she was writing, but it certainly contains worlds of knowledge.

More later.

May 30, 1963

Dear Gail:

The subject is "The Authority," which is a most interesting subject to me.

In the beginning I want to point out the workings of the human mind which have brought about the creation of the Authority. If I go on the deep end for the idea of enslavement, it means that I am pointing at those postulates which are made for other minds, including my own, for the purpose of holding me to a thought pattern, or the entanglement within the laws of the state, nation, religious, economical, political and other facets of life.

I want to point out here that the first factor of the mind lies in that direction of what everyone who knows the first principle of psychology: Every man is seeking to extract meaning from our environment, plus the fact that the pressures of his emotions are constantly being self-analyzed. To find a plausible reason for any confused state of mind or environment is mainly his goal. We want to know the why, how, and wherefore of the world that surrounds us. Our mind protests against chaos. From childhood we are asking WHY. So you see, this effort after meaning is broader than our impulsive tendency to rationalize and justify our immediate emotional state. Curiosity rumors result. Any odd-looking excavation in a city which has no explanation immediately will result in inspiring explanations of its purpose to curious minds.

This is where the authority was created. Someone will appear when the mind needs satisfaction to act as an authority to give answers, or the proper reading matter will fall in line. This is known as "The Authority," or the "Other Authority," or putting your dependence in another authority. He can actually be an authority upon the subject, a phony or a semi-ignorant person. It doesn't make any difference, but the point I am making is that: nobody should, under any circumstances, accept the word of a so-called authority provided he can work out his decisions or his own knowledge on whatever he is seeking. You see, what I am saying is simply this – everybody is telling us something these days; telling us how to vote, what to eat, what to wear, what to do with our leisure time, how to raise the children, what religion is best for you, what house you should purchase, et cetera. The authorities are numerous. For example, we have the physician who is an authority on health, disease and medicine; we have the priest who is the authority on salvation, spiritual happiness to name a few; we have the dietitian who is the expert on foods; the engineer who is able to construct buildings, and roads; the philosopher, teacher, politician, and a hundred others, besides the newspaper columnist who gives you the lowdown on the nation's ills, and a like number of things. It doesn't matter in which department of your life you may be lacking, there is someone who is the authority to tell you how to cure it.

Don't get me wrong! All I'm telling you is that everybody is ready, willing and able to advise you. If you seek advice from someone or want to get help from another be certain that you are satisfied to accept that advice. A real authority is reluctant to render his knowledge to others. The reason is that he wants the seeker to work out his answers. And this reminds me that a long time ago I went to Sudar Singh seeking advice, and he asked me this question: "Are you certain that you don't know the answer yourself?" He wouldn't tell me. My question was: "Are you my Master?" I had given him the story of seeing him out of the body several times and then repeated my question. His answer was the second time: "Go back to the Soul who appeared to you and ask him." My reply was: "I cannot see this Soul at my own desire, so how can I ask him?" He laughed at this question and the interview was ended.

The authority becomes the "They" like in the movie the other night. Once you challenge anyone on their source of authority, the answer will likely be "They told me," and this is to impress you that the informer is on the inside for getting special information which is to put you under a certain control, be it ever so slightly. This assignment to another authority is certainly one of the tendencies of the middle and lower classes in this country. Smarter people will assign their authority from a source book, an author, a celebrity, an article in the newspapers, a news writer, TV source or a religious leader, etc. There are people who can quote by the hour some sources from which they can impress others.

If you notice, many lecturers will use a set of other sources as their authority to back up their own authority. The listeners seem to demand this as a part of their prerogative for accepting the word of the speaker. Many politicians use this as their club to make their audience accept their word as authority; religious leaders do the same. For example, when JFK was in Nashville not long ago, he quoted from Socrates, Goethe, and other famed persons. Jesus used the Torah to quote as his authority – and Mohammed used the Old and New Testament; Buddha used the old Indian sacred scriptures. All use the other authority. Sudar Singh used the readings from the Sikh Bible and a few from the Indian scriptures in his nightly meetings. This is a pattern of all leaders and generally accepted for the use of making the listener take notice. The basic element in the technique goes something like this: "What I've just said is what Socrates said, and because I know it to be true and Socrates' words are backing me, then how can you doubt my word?"

This is the oldest gimmick in the world to get people into believing the individual who quoted it. However, I can point out that most people who use this technique are not thinkers in their own right. This is exactly what I'm trying to say to you. Do your own thinking. Let nobody tell you what and how to think – you can listen and if what they are saying has an element of truth within it then you can accept it. But how are you going to know that truth is being spoken to you? First, one must be detached from feeling and let his intuition take over, and secondly, one must be able to pick out the truth – in other words be discriminatory about what he wants to hear, and third, he must know the individual by reputation or personal friendship and that he speaks the truth at its best. This is perhaps a crude yardstick, but it is the best I can give you at this time and will serve until something better is ready for your next step.

"The Authority" is a strange but nebulous creature. He can be everywhere at once or looming so largely over a person that he literally swamps them. I have been so impressed by some people at times that it seems as though they gave me a gold coin, only to learn later it would more likelybe a lead or wooden nickel. Forgive me if I repeat myself but a Catholic priest once said to an audience in which I was sitting, that the westerners seem to lean so much upon another authority – true, for all answers lie within the individual. It needs patience and searching to get them out.

More later.

June 2, 1963

Dear Gail:

The subject is "Ridicule." Not exactly a spiritual subject but one you should know in order to protect yourself against and when necessary use it for protection against overaggressive persons.

Ridicule is: "The art or practice of exciting laughter at a person or thing by means of jesting, words, caricature, mocking, etc. Slightly contemptuous banter; A laughing matter; Of persons, a laughing stock, the butt of a joke; To laugh at someone or something in mockingly or disparagingly tone of voice."

The children of Ridicule are: Irony, Sarcasm, Satire, Scoffing, Mockery, Derision, Chaffing, Lampoon, Farce, Comedy, Buffoonery, and Practical Joke. I will take up the first three in detail with Ridicule. The definitions of these are as follows: Irony, is the form of ridicule in which a simulation of ignorance is displayed, (example: Socratic Irony). A sort of humor, ridicule or light sarcasm, the intended implication of which is the opposite of the literal sense of the words. A state of affairs or a result opposite to and as if in mockery of the appropriate result, e.g. the irony of fate – the use of wit to defeat another.

Sarcasm – A keen or bitter taunt; a cutting gibe or rebuke. The use of bitter, caustic or stinging remarks expressing contempt, often by ironical statement often framed in the language of wit. Satire – a poem or prose work holding up human vices, follies, etc., to ridicule or scorn. Trenchant (having a sharp edge or point, cutting, sharply clear, keen, mentally energetic) Wit – Irony or sarcasm, used for the purpose of exposing and discrediting vice or folly.

Another form of Ridicule is called Socratic Irony which is that form of irony invented by Socrates in his life 469-399 B.C. It is pretended ignorance or willingness to learn from others assumed for the sake of making their errors conspicuous by means of adroit (dexterous in use of mental facilities e.g., inventing lies on the spot, or excuses, or throwing up illusions before another) questioning. While on the subject of Socrates it is here I can give you his method of instruction. It was called the Socratic Method, which was the method of instruction used by the ancient Greeks, consisting of questionings the object of which is to elicit a consistent expression of something supposed to be implicitly known by all rational beings.

Now to go a little further in the subject of Ridicule, it is best to give you a briefing on wit, which is the power of reasoning and judgment in lively fancy which is amusing and humorous. A wit is usually a person quick in perception of felicitous and amusing associations of ideas or words and apt in expressing them. Wit is the power to evoke laughter; by evoking laughter showing swift perception of a situation or person's action. Humor is the ability to perceive the comical and absurd in human life or situations, usually without bitterness, and to express as others may see them in the following manner: (1) Irony, a way of speaking or writing in which the meaning is contrary to that seemingly expressed; (2) Sarcasm, a form of humor intended to wound feelings; (3) Satire, a type of writing that holds up vices or follies for ridicule and reprobation; (4) Repartee, the ability of answering quickly, pointedly and often wittily or humorously.

Science Fiction is so often used for the use of upholding the follies and vices of the human race – e.g., the writer's use of Irony. "The Marching Morons" is one of the finest examples of irony in science fiction. On the other hand Sinclair Lewis used satire in his novels, mainly "Main Street," and his story of evangelism "Elmer Gantry." Jonathan Swift was noted for his satire in his books e.g. "Gulliver's Travels," and "Tales of A Tub." On the other hand Alexander Pope kicked the people and his times with his poems of ridicule and satire. I forget the name of the famous dramatist whom he completely demolished with his satiric wit. Robert Benchley was a wit who could speak and write in the Socratic Irony Method, as was Will Rogers.

However, these forms of Ridicule are social weapons. They have no place except in this world of senses and matter, and are somewhat useful in the world of the psychic but not as much as this plane. The knowledge of Ridicule does however give you a method of discriminating truth from falseness. Most masters use all forms of it to get their disciples into thinking, into discipline; use it as a discipline or a method of driving the student into ambition for continuing on the path. It has all forms of good uses for mankind and very often a master will be as witty as Bob Hope in his talks with his own people. For example, I have often heard Sudar Singh use the expression "If two drunks can get together, why can't two people of God?" A use of Irony to emphasize his point. Of course Ridicule and Wit are the two levelers of the ego in a person, to bring an individual out of his vanity, to reduce him to nothing. Dorothy Parker, the poet who died a few years back, was a great wit. She could use the form of ridicule so stingingly that it would even hurt a dead man – e.g., when Calvin Coolidge died the word got to her when she was sitting in a theatre, her swift repartee was true to her reputation. When told she said, "How do they know he is dead?" Which is another form of scaling a person on the survival scale. Coolidge was actually so dead a person he could have been placed at 0.0. on the survival scale which is at death.

Here is a point you can watch. A person who is apt to use ridicule shows where he belongs on the survival scale easier than others. You can place him generally in the Anger Band, but he can belong in the Overt Hostility band, or in the Covert Hostility band. Ridicule is a form of aggressiveness caused by a person who has been badly hurt in the past, and an engram has been formed from his hurt, and repeated hurts which lock down the engram. Frustration often takes form in ridicule, saracasm or satire. The quickest way to drive a person into insanity is (1) Refusal to communicate with him and (2) Making use of the weapon of Ridicule upon him. A person can be reduced to complete nothingness by use of this insidious weapon, mainly because it can make you feel completely worthless, and when a person is reduced to a worthless stage he has lost his self-respect, his self-determination and his desire for improvement in life.

Ridicule is actually a tool to defeat people. But a necessary one when someone is driving you into defeat, and you can quickly turn the tables on him by a simple question like "Would you like to go to church with me, Sunday?" You counter with a question: "Think it would do you any good with God, or get you closer to heaven?"

Ridicule has its place but it is a weapon to watch closely in others, and to use only when needed for protection.

More later.

Letters to Gail

June 3, 1963

Dear Gail:

This letter is going off-beat for a change. I am going to sketch in background of the times so you can understand the forces which are pressing in upon you from the outside. I will discuss this time "Socialism." This is a political and economic theory of social organization based on collective or government ownership and democratic management of the essential means for the production and distribution of goods; it is also a policy or practice based on this theory.

On the extreme end of socialism we have it existing in Russia under the guise of communism, where all things are state owned, and the other side is a milder form in this country called democracy or liberalism. Here we have it in the form of unions, payroll deductions for (1) social security, (2) old age benefits, (3) federal taxes, (4) union dues, (5) sales taxes, (6) educational mill tax, (7) proposed old age medical benefits, (8) compulsory licensing of animals, autos, and a half-hundred laws on farming, industry, and business.

Socialism is that theory which was invented by Karl Marx and promoted through Friedrich Engels during the latter part of the 19th century. Both Jewish people put the theory together in the British Museum library and got it going in Germany. It is the socialistic forces which are to make the class struggle the fundamental force in history. Out of this came the socialistic disguise which made its attack upon capitalism and has pratically driven capitalism to its knees in the west. Socialism was adopted by England and it ruined her, along with World War I, and brought about the destruction of the English empire. It has such a hold upon the English people today that their food is rationed, they cannot change jobs unless necessary for health purposes, and only with a physician's notice to the government authorities, and lastly, an Englishman's home can be entered and searched without a warrant.

I am giving you this because this country is rapidly coming to the same level of ruin as England, if the trend keeps on going the same way it is now. Business and industry are rapidly becoming close to the edge with the payments made toward medical plans for their employees, and other benefits, plus the high salaries being paid out for labor. I am not against this; I only point it out that somewhere there must be a limit. I point out that our national budget was raised to the credit of several more billions of dollars again. Our gold reserve is rapidly dwindling. In the meantime the common man in the street is being taxed more and more. What is the result of this?

The public media, newspapers, magazines, television, radio, etc., have sold themselves out to the public issues. You never hear or read a brave newspaper or t.v. commentator criticize any of the powers that be anymore. They are afraid because they have sold themselves out for luxury – and body comfort – and without these they are completely in the cold, unhappy and have lost face. Also the churches have gone overboard for the socialistic form of life in these United States. It seems to be that nobody has the nerve to speak their voice because it might mean their income can be cut off and they are ostracized from society which means they have no way of making a living.

Good, bad or indifferent – I don't know what to tell you about this as a system to live under. But I do know that we are constantly getting new laws enforced on us which are cutting down our liberties. Briefly let me point out the various political systems under which we can live: Individualism; Democracy, Socialism, Totalitarianism, Nationalism, and Internationalism.

Now let's line this up against the spiritual life. What the clergy is preaching today is a socialistic paradise in which we will live in the hereafter in conformity with the laws of that world – so they say. Christianity says that we suffer here and have our happiness in the hereafter; Hinduism says we suffer in this life but are reincarnated as long as the problem is there, and then we go into heaven for the glorious reward. So taking advantage of the church teachings the socialists have preached to the people to suffer, suffer and have your reward in heaven; they preach that every man is alike and must be treated equally, and therefore the masses are homogeneous and all people are the same except themselves, and they live as they wish and make the laws. So by using the clergy, which is often a tool in the hands of the high politics, they control the people. If salvation is going to be the sameness of life as it is here, then who wants to spend eternity there?

Remember in one of my letters I pointed out that mass thought and belief could postulate a place in the Astral world? Well, then this is exactly what is taking place. When one of the religions forms a heaven for itself, modeled after the life on earth, socialism or anything else, then when the body dies the Jivatma goes to that place, if he belongs to that particular faith. I refer to this in The Tiger's Fang. *This is why I took so long to explain what was going on in the world today – and those who are of another culture or race will certainly gravitate to their own kind in the Astral world. You see they are not really free even after death – and this is the key to what is happening on Earth today, and the non-free persons. This is why there is so much disturbance going on within the Astral world, and why a large number of persons are returning in spirit form to try to tell those still in the body to change their ways or it'll be just as rough over there. If they in the spirit form can recognize this – but you must remember many cannot, though a few can – they come back to try to get the word across.*

This materialistic society is wrong, and there is going to be an upheaval one of these days because the mass of thought form will eventually force those forces of nature to go in reverse and like the ancient continent of Atlantis will go down into the ocean. Only a few thousand will be able to get away. Certain mediums have been preaching this for years, and there is an inkling of truth in their statements. How much I cannot say, but it is bound to come, not because the moral downfall of man has come about, but because he has forced it with his atom bomb explosions which have disturbed the atom chain, and other natural powers, as well as other mass energies which have been released on this planet.

This isn't a scare letter, but it is to make you aware of what is going on around you. Remember the general person is quite ignorant of these forces which have upset the economic, social and natural lives of all peoples. This is why I have kept pointing out to you that this is a warring universe, and man must get off of it or else he comes to self-destruction; otherwise he must learn to leave his body, at will, and be free of all these inflows of destructive energy upon him. The body means nothing, and therefore one should not allow it to be his main goal – its upkeep, pampering, and its comforts. Socialism means to hinder those who believe in freedom of mind and spirit. It certainly doesn't want anyone to be able to get out of the body for this means freedom!

More later.

Paul

Letters to Gail

June 4, 1963

Dear Gail:

Now I leave the mental and intellectual subjects behind and for the next 25 letters—to the end of this series—will dwell on spiritual themes.

This letter will be on the Names of God. It might be better if I said the Secret Names of God, for not many people know the names of God, let alone the secret names. A short story entitled "The Nine Billion Names of God," by Arthur Clarke, illustrates this point. It's a story about a Lama in Tibet, ordering a western Univac to count up the names of God. It went to pieces after nine billion count.

God has a different name in each religion on this planet, and a different one for each different religion on all other planets. It has a different name on each of the planes and grand divisions through which you travel to reach the highest world. In Christianity It has a poetic name called God, taken from the old Greek term deity. Often in the Christian cults It is given several names: Incorporeal, Divine, Supreme, Infinite, Mind, Spirit, Soul, Principle, Life, Truth, Love, etc. The Hindu uses the name Brahma, Parabrahma, and OM. Allah is the Muslim word for it. Rama is an ancient Indian name; others are: Nam, Para-Ishwar, Param Atma, Param Akshar, Nirankar, Nirala, Ormuzd (Old Persian and Parsee term), Ishwara, Hari Ray, Ahura Mazda (Zoroaster's name for God).

In the world of saints, God is expressed by many words such as Swami, Ekankar, Akal, Nirala, Anami, Agam, Alakh, Sat Purusha, Prabhu, Prabhswami, Akshar, Paramakshar, Purusha, etc. There are as many names for God as there are ideas. Even the American Indians had a name for It which was Mana. Usually the word Anami is used for God which means Nameless. Akal means timeless, and Nirala means peerless, having none like him. Agam is a name for It meaning inaccessible.

God is the Anglo-Saxon adaptation of Good. Deus is the Latin name, signifying something like supreme emperor. Theos is the Greek appellation, meaning the chief of those august powers who sat upon Mount Olympus and ruled the world. Adonai, or Elohim, or Yahveh, are some of the Hebrew names assigned to the God who was the first tribal deity of the Jews, but was later proclaimed Lord over all gods and worlds. He was the supreme law-giver, the commander of all the armies of Israel. He was the majestic warrior whose wrath was so much to be feared.

The Norsemen had their Thor, and modern Indian students are fond of the terms Akshar, Paramakshar, Purusha and Purushottama. Other names are Pani (Urdu), Eau (French), but regardless they all mean the same. In spite of all this confusion regarding names and characteristics among the gods, there is a golden thread running through all scriptures which concerns the central idea of a great, over-ruling power that is greater and better than man.

Many times the divine Nam, or Sound, or Word stands for all that God is or has ever said or done. It includes all of Its qualities. As said in previous letters it means that it is the only way in which the Universal Spirit can manifest Itself into human consciousness. When the Supreme Being manifests Itself as Sat Nam, in the plane of Sach Khand, meaning true home, the highest plane in the fourth grand division, It becomes fully personified, embodied, individualized, for the first time and brings into manifestation all the qualities of deity. As Sat Nam It becomes the personal Creator, Lord, God, and Father. There It becomes the fountain out of which the Audible Life Stream proceeds. When man hears it, he hears God; when he feels it, he feels God.

Known to many as Sat Purusha, then the Supreme Being, is called the positive power, because he rules the whole of creation from the positive end of all the universe of universes. Now this Sat Purusha is often called the highest of all manifestations, but he is not, for the Spirit first manifests Itself as Sat Nam. However, the races upon the lower planes generally regard this manifestation Sat Purusha, which is below the Sat Nam manifestation, as the Supreme Creator. Even the saints often regard Sat Purusha as the supreme being for below him no member of the grand hierarchy has power to create. They have creative powers over everything else, but no power to create a Jivatma, and no power to destroy the Jivatma. Now in Sach Khand, under the Sat Nam, and within the Sat Nam, if you can understand this paradox, the Sat Purusha has established his throne at the very gates of the lower border of the fourth grand division.

This deity is that Lord with whom the masters must have all their undertakings in carrying out their sacred mission of returning the Jivatmas to the Sat Desha region. To him all subordinates pay homage, and from him all take orders. He is the supreme Father, the Supreme Light Giver, of all saints. He is the God that we know, and here is where the devotion of all people belongs, for he is the real Lord of all worlds in existence. Alakh Purusha and Agam Purusha, and the Nameless One, the Universal, Sat Nam, and those above him are so utterly incomprehensible, so fathomless and impersonal, that none can approach them, even in thought. But Sat Purusha stands mid-way between the Infinite Light and the created universe.

The Supreme Being is called by various names in different languages, but the eastern mystics have known him as HU, an Arabic name, the natural name, not a man-made name; the only name of the Nameless, which all nature proclaims. This is the secret name of God. This name is derived from the word HU, the most sacred of all sounds. I think it is derived by a Sufi word but it actually doesn't belong to any language, but no language can help belonging to it. This alone is the true name of God, a name that no people and no religion can claim as their own. The word is uttered not only by human beings, but is repeated by animals and birds. All things and beings exclaim this name of the Lord; for every activity of life expresses distinctly this very sound.

Whatever one might think the nine billion names of God actually exist; but there is only one HU. This is the true name of the Absolute, and is that which the true seeker comes to know sooner or later. If he passes the throne of Sat Purusha, and goes beyond God, then he will come to know this secret name, for he will be given it as the password of the worlds beyond God. One cannot think in terms of these beyond worlds, but in their existence there is never a physical sense used, for these faculties have long been dropped and the Jivatma now exists in the world of intuition. There are actually no words in which to describe these experiences.

More later.

Letters to Gail

June 6, 1963

Dear Gail:

The subject is "Intuition," sometimes called Cognition. This is extremely important for it means that the subject is the language in which the Absolute communicates with many of ITS subjects throughout the planes of the universes.

Remember, this is one of the most significant studies you can make, and it would do well for you to go beyond this letter in reading up on it, or making a practice of your own to find out about the other world through your intuition of psychic senses. The use of the intuition is not easy for it is only when one can set aside his physical senses and allow the inflow of the psychic senses can he then make contact with that which is beyond or the use of PSI. This is in a way hard to do, but once anyone catches the point it can be mastered. But there is another factor involved in the matter – how far can one trust the psychic senses, and how much is he deluding himself in trusting them?

Cognition is the word I'll use instead of intuition. Cognition is the art or faculty of thinking or reflecting effortlessly. An idea or thought flashing into your mind – the power of knowing, or the knowledge received without recourse to inference or reasoning. When you have a flash of cognitive thought, or your inner senses speak without you realizing, a truth or direction for you to follow, it is best to listen and follow. You know it is truth. This is why those certain people who are followers of God can live so closely to IT and follow IT regardless; they know and recognize truth when it is spoken to them.

There is a word used for this art which you should know. Intuitionism: Ethically it is the doctrine that moral values are intuitively apprehended. In philosophy it means – the doctrine that there are self-evident truths intuitively known, which form the basis of human doctrine. Then it is described as the doctrine that the objects of perceptions are intuitively known to be real.

Inspiration is often used for the same resulting effects. Other names are insight, perceptivity, instinct, association, apprehension, premonition, presentiment, clairvoyance, sixth sense, extrasensory perception, second sight, hunch, innate, and apperception. There are a half-hundred names used for the ability to gather the spiritual data through the inner senses. Poetry and music are said to be the closest to this faculty because they are written from the inner senses. So much poetry is taken out of the reactive bank although today it is called great poetry. So much of the music is of the same nature, although it is the so-called great music of our times. All popular music and popular poetry are animalistic and have no place from out of the true cognitive arts. So few of the arts are written from the inner senses although they might be thought to have been done this way. I cannot in any way condone the greatness of poetry and music unless it is of the highest quality – taken straight from the heart of the Absolute.

The way to travel the road of cognition is by stilling the senses. One of the great Psalms, the 46th has a line, number 10, which goes like this: "Be still and know that I am God." This is the great technique of the art of knowingness. It is probably the most wonderful phrase in the Bible. It really is the whole Bible in a nutshell. The current of human thought is hurrying every individual along to its own ends, and it seems much easier to swim with it by accepting difficulties, by rehearsing grievances, by dwelling upon symptoms, than to draw resolutely away from these things, and contemplate the Absolute, which is one way out of trouble, one way to make contact with the Absolute through the inner senses.

Therefore one must train himself to rise above this hurrying tide of error – for error is always hurried; to sweep one off his feet is its master strategy, and turning the back upon conditions, however bad they may seem. Be Still and Know that I am God, is the answer. This is not the action of doing nothing, but to be actively passive. It is to know that God is God. Such stillness is the reverse of laziness or inaction. The still dwelling upon the Absolute is the quietest but the most potent action of all. Of course to be afraid is to have more power in the evil than in the Lord! Remember this all the days of your life!

One of the best examples of writings which have come out of the inner senses today is that of Thomas Merton, in a book called The Seeds of Contemplation! *This is a worthy study for anybody to see what he has gathered from the Voice of Silence as Madame Blavatsky, founder of Theosophy, calls that Voice of God. Her book by the same title is worth your time to look up and study. It is a small book and will be that which can give you much comfort in learning to make contact with the*

Absolute. One of the interesting points about intuitional dialogues with the Absolute is how much the listener is led into thinking that he is in contact with the Almighty.

So many times this isn't true. His reactive bank may be whispering to him; an entity on the other side may be posing as the true voice, or one of the minor gods on the spiritual ladder might be speaking, or it could be a Master. If you know anything about the characteristics of the signs of the zodiac, you being a Cancer type, you can tell a great deal about who is talking to the individual from the inner self. For example, many times the dialogue will be exactly what is expected from the reactive bank, in that it is repeating all the characteristics of the Cancer type traits. Now take for example, Joan of Arc, who heard voices direct her to take up the leadership of France, or George Fox, who founded Quakerism. These people, if I remember right, were born under the Aquarius or Pisces sign. Both are close to the religion type individual, and the reactive bank falling under the influence of the planets in the Zodiac sign (as the ones named above) will whisper or speak out loud to the individual – or at least he believes that he has heard a voice directing him what to do. One of the best examples of this type of voice speaking to the individual is in the preface to Saint Joan of Arc, by Bernard Shaw – that is one of his famous plays. Although I don't care for George Bernard Shaw, this is a good study made of St. Joan and voices.

I've had the experience of having voices direct me what to do. In some cases they were correct in their direction, other times completely wrong. I cannot tell you whether they were true or not, but I believed they were – and that's what counted with me. Tis said that schizophrenics have such experiences; however, I'm not in position to say that I'm one, or that they do – but the experience is actually so real that anyone experiencing it has no doubt. Anyway, I think it's useful even for humor, as when George Fox was ordered to take off his hat while in the presence of Cromwell, dictator of England, replied by saying, "God told me not to take my hat off to anybody but Him!" And he got away with it! Interesting point, eh?

More later.

June 9, 1963

Dear Gail:

It is only in the human form that the astral and mental bodies are fully developed. Therefore, even when the Jivatma has gross-consciousness and is unconscious of the astral and mental, it does work through the astral (another name for feeling) and mental selves, not directly but on the material plane.

Even so, if the gross-conscious Jivatma is unconscious of the feeling and mental sides of itself, and does not realize energy and mind, it can use energy through various aspects of mind – such as thoughts, desires and emotions.

In the human-form when the Jivatma has subtle-consciousness (astral cognition) it is unconscious of the gross body and mental bodies, yet it does work through the body and mind, not directly, but on the astral plane. So even if the astral-consciousness Jivatma in human form is not conscious of the body and therefore doesn't realize the gross body and the mind, it can use the body, through various aspects of the body, as eating, drinking, sleeping, seeing, feeling, and it can use the mind through various aspects of the mind, as thoughts, desires and emotions.

This is certainly possible for if the Jivatma is working from the astral plane, and has a human body through which it can operate on the physical, it will often stay in the astral but run the human body on the other side of the veil – another invisible barrier. You find many older persons who seem vague, incoherent and lackadaisical are in this state – the Jivatma is living in the astral, having gone there, but refuses to give up the body through the mind, feeling and senses. It wishes to keep contact with this world. There are people – young, middle-aged and old – who are in this state. They are beyond the invisible barrier as themselves but still run their bodies on this side.

These people are known as Masts in India, and to get them in one place or the other is the duty of many masters. The masters realize that the Jivatma learns something which is not good for itself or mankind. It learns swiftly that the power of energy is easily harnessed, and can be used for a number of things, i.e., raising the dead, giving sight to the blind, or limbs to the maimed, or destroying the bodies of mankind, used by other Jivatmas. It can wield tremendous powers over the physical world, including the nuclear energies. Where the Master is concerned is that the astral-conscious Jivatma who has become powerful through its knowledge of harnessing energy (called electronic power sometimes) is in danger of sliding down to the lowest level of consciousness while making conscious use of its energy in the form of miraculous powers.

When the Jivatma reaches this state, it can be at any of the three planes within the first grand division. But now something has happened. A state of confusion may arise for it has noble intentions but is like Don Quixote who had a muddled mind and saw enemies in windmills and recognized ignorant peasant girls as princesses. Its conceptions of the physical universe and its laws are now topsy-turvy, and it is forced to recognize a new philosophy of life which it never thought existed. The laws which helped it to soar upward through the planes can also be those laws which can send it tumbling to the bottom of the planes again.

When the Jivatma reaches the stage of the consciousness of the fourth plane, still within the first grand division, it experiences the realization of tremendous energy of the astral world. Thus it can go up into the mental world or be kept at this particular point. Thus the Jivatma is on the threshold of the mental world, commanding the cosmic energy at its height, and thus is more susceptible to the overpowering forces of the mind, namely, the thoughts, desires and emotions. And although this astral power-conscious Jivatma on the fourth plane consciously makes use of the subtle world's energy at its zenith, it is still unconscious of Mind. It therefore unconsciously makes use of the aspects of mind, which are now too overpowering and thus most alluring for the Jivatma which, so to speak, has to face and bear the full blast of the aspects of the mind (thoughts, desires and emotions) at their highest.

This situation for the human atma on the fourth plane is extremely dangerous, since it is extremely treacherous. Here the Jivatma, equipped with highest energy, which can be put to use either for the best or for the worst, has to maintain a sort of equilibrium of two forces at their zenith, i.e., the height of energy of the astral world and the overpowering heights of the aspects of the mental world. If the Jivatma, while in this position, unconsciously uses the aspects (thoughts, desires and emotions), it then cannot resist using the energy at its climax for the worst by performing powerful miracles to satisfy its own overpowering desires. It is even capable of creating the whole world of forms with all of its creation, so great is the power obtained from the energy at its height of which this astral-conscious Jivatma is conscious.

Many veiled warnings are given to the initiate, e.g., "dabbling in the occult often brings trouble and destroys the operator." It needs moral courage and even daring to attempt to use the occult secrets on the mundane plane. Knowledge applied wrongly can bring results which can be the ruin of the operator. This is why it is pointed out to find the Master who can keep watch over the seeker. This is why the moral training of the individual is needed so badly from the beginning – e.g., Hitler who used this until he began to misuse those strange laws which man doesn't ordinarily know. The law itself uses each man's personal weakness to destroy him. Any man who misuses the strange magnetism that is given him at this state to sway the emotions of women and subject them to his will is eventually destroyed through some woman. A man greedy for riches is allowed to amass them, and then the possession of those riches becomes the sword that strikes him down – or with millions at his command, he is placed in a position where no sum of money can help him.

The ordeal of the Jivatma at this position in his journey is to recognize this, for the sharp edge of the law, like the Sword of Damocles, will make him confront his weakness, and conquer it or be conquered. This is the reason why I have not given you much about Scientology – it can bring the individual to this point, but without moral training, or control. The Jivatma who realizes how much energy it can harness can blow up the universe, i.e., the scientist or politician who has control of the deadly hydrogen bomb – but the Jivatma doesn't need the mechanics of engineering – it does it through the invisible by the same methods of healing another. This is why the initiate is always watched by a master, to keep from wrecking his spiritual career through the misuse of his spiritual powers. Often if the Jivatma is about to lose control of itself, its powers are snatched away by the Master, who can control the minds of all astral-conscious and gross-conscious Jivatmas. The cases of actual downfall are rare and occur as exceptions to the rule for those under the Master. But it takes calm of self, and to keep from growing into vanity and to keep from becoming panicked in the face of all these powers. I rather think that this was the experience which Adam and Eve must have had in the Garden of Eden. Eve, coming into the realization of the powers of the other worlds, had it pointed out by Satan, the advantages of making use of these powers, and therefore had sexual intercourse with him, releasing the power of creativity in and through the gross body thus lowering the consciousness to the gross-body and putting the energy into the world through this channel – instead of direct use for uplifting of the Jivatma and those around her. Hence, she liked the pleasure of sexual activity and lured Adam into it, and God drove them out of the fourth plane into the material plane where they would always have to create through the material-gross body, instead of making a direct manifestation of their creation. And all this done because Satan knowing what would happen gave him gross bodies on Earth for his playthings, and trapping the Jivatmas within the gross-bodies.

This is theory but it rather makes some sense to me, for to release the tremendous energies for anything other than help for those in distress or the race as a whole, will bring disaster upon the operator. Therefore, why couldn't it have happened to Adam and Eve as well as anyone who followed them thereafter in this world?

More later.

Letters to Gail

June 10, 1963

Dear Gail:

The subject is "The Lofty Teachings." The Lofty Teachings are not always secret; it's that the mass cult man doesn't look at them in the proper way. He isn't interested in knowing what might be given him in the esthetical way, while he is still in the body.

When one rises above the consciousness of the body, then he may find many different viewpoints of spiritual matters which had never occurred to him heretofore. Yet the teachings are secret – a paradox as usual – which is always existent in the spiritual truths. Spiritual Truth itself is a paradox, and you must come to know it in this manner until you are ready to accept; then suddenly you know that Truth is not a paradox, but it was yourself who was the paradox – and you were looking at it in that manner.

The Lofty Teachings are those of the saints, saviors and savants. They are the pure utterances which dropped from the lips of these higher ones. You can be assured of the fact that none ever were able to take down the utterances of Christ, Buddha and other saviors without coloring them. St. Paul was one of the worst for putting his own interpretation into the words of Jesus. You find that no disciple ever wrote the pure truth – but wanted to use the gospel as his own to the development of personal power – and, yet, so many disciples of so many saviors have this ambition. If you are at all in doubt, study the history of the Catholic Church – it has one of the worst examples of the development of power in the history of this world. Buddha's disciples wanted to do the same but were kept from it by the fact that the Buddha had foreseen this and made rules to hold down any personal ambition among the generations to come who worshipped the Buddha. However, Tibet was a place where the politics of power reigned in the Buddhist monasteries, and the King's regents have always been great political powers – when I speak of the King's regents – I mean the Dalai Lama.

The Lofty Teachings will contain, as the basic principle, the Sound Current. You will find this teaching in every mystery teaching in the world. If it is not there you can be assured that the teaching is not a true teaching, and if the teacher doesn't recognize or give any sufficient reason for not recognizing it, then you can be certain that he is not aware of it, nor does he recognize it. I am sure that almost every mystic teaching does give the Sound Current. Some of those who are not aware of the Sound Current are: Spiritualism, Orthodox Christianity, Islam, Swedenborgism, and a few others with which you have probably by now become acquainted.

Since the Sound Current comes from the center of all things, then it is the essence of the Lofty Teachings. Tulsi Das, one of the great Masters, during the middle ages was a true follower of the Lofty Teachings; so was Shamus-i-Tabriz, one of the greats whom many do not know, yet his name will keep creeping up throughout all the history of the true teachings. This individual was gifted with the ability to leave his body at will, for he could come and go at will. Once when he heard that four assassins were going to kill him at a certain place, he left his body and appeared to them. When they tried to stab him and their knives stuck nothing, it frightened them so badly they gave up to the police, asking for protection. He lived in Persia, during the eighth century B.C., and there left a few scattered teachings. I have some in my notes.

Now one of the most interesting points at this particular stage is to discuss briefly what the metaphysicians keep talking about, that is – the we-feeling, the we-ness of all. You have noticed this as an expression in people's dialogues. "We must accept this principle, or we suffer the consequence!" This is typical of their thinking – which is typical of this century. There is no usness in the higher planes – we do not exist as a togetherness like McCall's Magazine of Togetherness program. It is simply that we don't exist as most people think – and as many of the beginners in spiritual training believe. There is a first experience of the cosmic path in which the individual sees himself as a part of all. But the mistake is that he gathers to himself the thought that we is the basis of this experience. It certainly isn't, for the experience has only gained him an insight into the area of getting into the astral plane – but just a little way – not completely inside.

The feeling of universality, being all in one and one in all, is false – rather a deceptive state of cosmic understanding. You and I, speaking in the terms of oneness, must understand that it is the "I" that counts, and not being a member of a team. The individual must be that which is the ultimate ending. In other words, the closer the individual comes to God, or the Absolute, the more individualistic he becomes. It is only that person (the Jivatma) who is sunk in this materialistic universe who wants to include all in his own problems or his troubles by saying that "We must abide by this law, because it helps all!" You must realize that that person is trying to include you as his contemporary because he is troubled and wants the companionship of another to share his mood. Remember the article on Yang and Yin.

The closer that one comes to the Absolute, I repeat again, the more individualistic he becomes. The more individualistic one becomes in his thinking and in his closeness to the Absolute, the lonelier he becomes. He doesn't speak in the terms of we anymore for he is accepting the full load of the responsibility of his own karma, or the duties laid upon him through his actions. He is the highest of individuals! The Absolute doesn't train Its favorite children to become automatics like the materialistic world does. He who is favored by God to become the true child of God is a complete individualistic person, I mean, Jivatma. A person may act as if he is an individual, but if you look at him closely you might find that he is actually a person bound by the cords of materialism and he is struggling to get loose, and his eccentricities are not true freedom. I rather doubt if you will find over a half-dozen true individuals in your lifetime – those who have true freedom.

Therefore the individual Jivatma is that one who can do as he pleases, go where he pleases and act as he pleases under all circumstances. He can be free of any action, yet he can indulge in it without losing himself to its entangling coils – like food, sex, or any of the passions. He can be angry but he is not lost in anger but mocks-up anger because the position demands it and it is expected of him. He acts in any capacity desired merely because the position demands it, but it has nothing to do with him inwardly.

All who follow the Lofty Teachings recognize them by intuition and never have to struggle over what they may be. He knows by trusting his inner senses, and can give them the test; he is versed in the art of knowledge of the esoteric teachings and will be able to disperse them to others without cost, or any reward.

More later.

June 12, 1963

Dear Gail:

The subject is "Sight Without Eyes." This may well prove to be your most important subject. This is seeing those entities, things and objects behind the curtain which separates this world from the next. It isn't hard once you understand and know how it is done; once you look into eternity as you said, the other night, of having done.

Blake, the poet, had this ability of seeing what others couldn't see. St. Catherine of Siena, a 14th century saint, tells of seeing Jesus and the princes of the apostles, Peter, Paul and St. John, over the church of her faith, during her childhood. St. Francis of Assisi saw and spoke to his Lord. Mohammed saw and spoke with the Angel Gabriel. St. Joan of Arc saw and spoke with two saints of the church and was promised victory if she would lead the armies of France against the English. Seeing behind the curtains of the veil one is called a clairvoyant – if one can hear the voice he is clairaudient.

This is not an unusual gift in people, for hundreds of people can do this including yourself provided you would make the effort. The key to the psychology of the visionary (often called the saint) are the words of Jesus in which he said: "He that heareth my commandments and keepeth them, he it is who loveth me. And I will love him and manifest myself to him." These words seem to bring out the gift of seeing without eyes in the individual. When one can accept them then he is able to see the Christ or any of his disciples and the angels, can hear the angels and those wondrous ones on the other side speaking to him.

In order to see one cannot be passive and wait for the vision to come to him. He must go out and seek the vision – it is similar to the going after something in the physical. One must go to it, in order to receive whatever he is seeking. Now the same applies here – if you wish to see the Lord, or any of those on the other side, then it is a simplicity in the way of doing so. You must see whatever you wish to see; let it be there standing before you, protecting you from that which you do not wish to have about you. A simple test is to look at the buildings on the corner; then make the image in your mind that instead of the buildings you are looking at a bare lot. If you are strong enough to see this, then you can go to the next step: that of seeing something you wish in your door, before you, or near you. For example, if you look without strain (now is the time to become passive) at the side of the wall in the room, and want to see me there, you can image up the picture so strongly that I am standing there. And this image can be so strong that you can draw my psychic body there to speak with you.

I once asked Sudar Singh how it was that he could be in the presence of a large number of people all over the world at the same time. Instead of giving me a bit of flummery like most Gurus will, he explained it logically by saying that whoever wished to see him, could see him, but they must draw up that image in their own creative-mind, and that image of him belongs personally to the individual. It isn't anyone else's picture. By establishing this image so strongly in the individual's own mind, by the individual, he could call up the imagery at will, and by filling this imagery with electronic solidness, it becomes real and can move about, have life, talk and even feel solid. This is all drawn out of the spirit, and is actually a part of the Master himself; real, but unreal – solid, yet unsolid, but always truth.

This inner communion with the Master, or some higher entity is necessary. The words Entriamo nella cella del coqnocimento di noi, *apply here. It is latin for the phrase: "Let us enter into the cell of knowledge." Once the Christ said to St. Catherine, "Many live in the cell, and yet in their thoughts they are outside it. I will, therefore, that thy cell shall be the knowledge of thyself."*

This was the knowledge of self – and the knowledge of God. She talked constantly to the Christ and his apostles. Her conclusion of self-knowledge was that she must remain in the cell of self-knowledge and understand that she was not, but that all being is of God. This is an interesting point because it gives one the insight that while being the individual he becomes that which has ability to see and communicate with the higher deity. The passive virtues: humility, selflessness, frugality, abstemiousness, spring from this knowledge of self. These passive virtues are necessary in the ability of sight without seeing. This one must have before gaining the knowledge of God; and after seeing the Absolute and after communication with him, then one gains the active virtues which are: unassuming, cosmic viewpoint, sparing of thought and goods, temperate, and large in giving self and goods to others. Generally aggressive in thought and deed against that which is not of God.

Once you have looked upon the face of the Absolute there is no turning back; once you have communicated with him, there is no turning away. He makes his claim upon you, and you are always his. You will thereafter see and talk with him at his leisure; you are the chosen one, and you, like a child who must see its Father at times, will have need of seeing the Absolute. You will become like the city that is set upon a hill, as stated in the Bible – which cannot be hid. You cannot hide yourself for you will always be in the midst of things, be in the heart of all matters which concern themselves with mankind, if not physically, with your mind and feelings. The supernatural gift is yours provided you look to your self to find it, to see without sight. The best policy is that you must take the stand that you can do this, and once assumed it will become natural. You must feel this way. "Father, in Thee I am, in Thee I move and live, whether I am awake or asleep, whether I speak or write." This is the attitude in which you must live in order to see the Lord, or lords of the universe and have your contact with them, and be in them.

There are two kinds of love in man: the love of the Absolute and of his beloved and the love of the world. There are two wills, the will of the Absolute and self-will. One of these two forces, love of the world, of self-will, leads to interior unrest, unhappiness, everything distrustful and everlasting loss. The other, love of the Absolute, will lead to a different sort of restlessness, a feeling of reaching peace and health of the Jivatma, and everlasting life. These two loves are not easy to acquire, and keep for one's self. The love of the self is not easy, for generally man has a hatred for himself – he must love himself first before he can love anything else.

I desire that you take up the chance of having sight without eyes. That wherever you look you can see the object of your religious or spiritual desire. That you can blank out everything else in your vision and see only what you wish to seek. You have the ability to do this easily. You must make this step now; don't wait for tomorrow – and once you do suddenly those things which look like people become queer to you – they are not normal for you are now living in the other worlds with your feet on the Earth. You can see and hear both worldly things and heavenly things.

More later.

Letters to Gail

June 15, 1963

Dear Gail:

The subject is "The Angel of Death." Although this is not as important an item as some of the others you have had, or to come, it will enlighten you on the proposed ideas which you have brought up now and then in our conversations.

At onset I'm going to give you a number of Great Ideas which have affected mankind. (1) Buddhism, (2) Hinduism, (3) Confucianism, (4) The Wheel, (5) The Axe, (6) Communism, (7) Democracy, (8) Individualism, (9) Socialism, (10) The Atomic Theory, (11) The Libido Theory of Freud, (12) Demonism or Satan in the medieval ages, (13) American Revolution, (14) Jewish sacred literature, (15) Original Sin, (16) Industrial Revolution, (17) Marxism, (18) Christianity, (19) Matriarch, (20) Patriarch, and (21) Man's communion with the other worlds or God. Of course I could have included a number of others like Zoroastrianism, and a large number of others but they are ideas which you will pick up under one grand total of what I might call the Great Father Image – or the God Theory.

These are not in order but they have affected the course of history – for history is hardly anything more than the deeds of men which have been recorded someway or other. Generally it is propaganda but you might be able to sift the good from the bad and make it possible for understanding. This is why the religionists claim that God made this universe and went off to leave it to its own ends. This is why most religions have a fatalistic point of view, e.g., the pulpit bangers yell "Do it the way I say or God will take care of you – and it won't be pleasant!" You have a choice of doing what you want and generally wind up far ahead of the herd who believed what some jolly-talker said from the pulpit.

To get along with the subject on the Angel of Death, I now start. The Angel of Death is supposedly that being which stands on the other side of the barrier and gives you an accounting of your earthly behavior so you will be sent to the proper assignment in the afterlife. Some state that it is God that does this – but anyone with ordinary sense couldn't conceive of God doing this for he is an exalted being who gives out assignments to others, his servants, to do. Nor is this Entity St. Peter who stands at the gates of Paradise to check over our records. Neither would St. Peter be so low on the scale of prestige in the other world.

Immediately after the Jivatma passes away he is taken by the messengers of death to the subtle regions where Dharam Ray, the righteous judge, sits enthroned to judge every individual according to his deserts. That is unless you have become trained to by-pass this entity, or if a Master or relative who is acquainted with the procedure in the world can take you past. In Christianity these messengers of death are very appropriately called the Angels of Death or the Dark Angels for they are indeed dark and that is why many of the caricatures of death put the entities in dark clothing and why they look like skeletons with sickles. In India these entities are called Yama dutas or the messengers of Yama, the king of the dead. This judge is always in court to take care of arrivals at his door. There is no long waiting, no sitting in a jail cell.

No one questions the judgment which is handed down to him, and there is no comment, no long-winded oratory for the defense, no pretended righteous condemnation of the prosecution, for the prisoner knows that his karma has earned him the justice handed down. He is to be taken to that place, region or condition, where he has earned his residence, be that good or bad. He will remain there for a fixed time according to the judgment rendered and handed down to him. After that has expired, he is then returned to this world, or some other world, to begin a new life. He may enjoy a rest in some heaven, or paradise, some pleasant country, perhaps many times more beautiful and delightful than any portion of this world. There he may remain for a year, a thousand or a million years, all depending upon his karma. The higher he goes on the other planes, the longer the period of his residence there. If he returns then he may well be put on a planet other than this earth world.

If his life has been one of a lower order, he may be taken to some purgatory, or reformatory, often called hell, there to endure the punishment earned by him during his lifetime. If his life has been one of gross misdeeds, of cruelty and greed, of murder and robbery, of slander and debauchery, he cannot escape punishments; however all punishments are remedial – they are intended for his good, to produce a reformation of character – but they are not eternal as Christianity always emphasizes. The punishments may be severe or mild, according to the earnings of the individuals who receive them. Everyone must pay off their karmic debts somewhere be it in the afterlife or in this life, or in the lives of their own incarnations.

But even going to these places there is no such thing as despair, no hopeless finality. There is kindness given should one deserve it, for the Absolute never forsakes anyone, not even in his darkest hour. This period of darkness is that which the seeker must endure or go through when he is striving desperately on the pathway to God. St. John of the Cross gives this in a very vivid poem called "The Dark Night of Soul." Once the seeker of God has crossed this area of purgatory he never has to return again – even Christ spent three days in hell, during his death, following the cross – which is given in the Bible.

One must remember that a Master working under the directions of the Supreme Power administers the karma of his disciple. From that hour forward, the negative power, under which the Angel of Death operates – and the Judge of the Dead, has nothing to do with his accounts and has no power or control over him. The agents of death cannot approach him, nor can he ever be called into the courts of the Dharam Ray for judgment. His destiny in this life and the next rests entirely in the hands of his Guru. The Master administers the karma of his disciple as he thinks best for him.

Where the church is wrong about the meting of good and bad rewards in the afterlife is they claim that one must wait for the judgment day. This is wrong for this court is held immediately upon death and the Jivatma is given his accounting, and assigned. Secondly, there are those who have received the initiation from a living Master, but done little or nothing in the way of spiritual exercises. After death this individual is met by the Master and assigned by him to a training school where they make good progress under his direction. When ready for higher worlds the Master will advance them. The third class, those who have done well under the Master, is met by the Master and taken to the region he's earned. Neither class will return to Earth again, or other worlds for reincarnations. However, if you have earned the knowledge of going in and out of your body at will you will not face the Judge of the Dead, but will go to that world you have earned. You can also meet people after their death and escort them through the gates into their earned places.

More later.

Letters to Gail

June 16, 1963

Dear Gail:

The subject is the "Seat of Knowledge." Without doubt this will be one of the most important letters you've yet received. You must understand that the Seat of Knowledge is that Absolute which directs Its knowledge toward all who are willing to listen – hence the letter on Intuition. Several letters will tie in with this one, and it wouldn't hurt you to go back and reread the Names of God, Spiritual Hierarchy, and maybe the one on the different types of mysticism. The rereading of these would give you a better background on the subject I am now about to discuss. You will begin to see how the pattern of the spiritual falls together.

The Seat of Knowledge is in the highest plane sometimes called the Sat Lok, or the Sat Desha region, which is the region of the Universal Spirit. The Lord of the lowest region, whose name is Sat Purusha, radiates a light from himself, equal to the light of a million suns like our own, but who can form a mental picture of it. Below this Great Entity is Sat Nam, the first manifesting form for the Jivatma to have any contact in communication, but it is the former from which arises all the great knowledge of the Absolute, and which is the Throne of God, out from which flows the fountain as spoken of in Revelations, by John of Patmos. Since the Absolute must descend from the rarified atmosphere where the region is completely pure and nothing can come near him there, he manifests himself in a sense in the Sat Purusha which is the Seat of Knowledge and through which he must send downward through the planes that God-knowledge which will be caught by certain individuals and used for the benefit of all.

Since so few on this earth plane can make contact with this Seat of Knowledge, we must have the Masters who can make the contact and who can give us Truth in its rarer form. This is the reason for the theory that every thousand years a savior comes to this earth because he must reteach these truths and how to make contact with them. The knowledge which flows out from this Seat of Divine Wisdom must ride the Audible Life Stream, like fishes do when being carried downstream in a rapids, or a rushing stream toward the ocean. Only this is in reverse. It comes out of that majestic ocean of life and love, which we know as the Absolute, first channeled through Sat Purusha, which acts as the fountainhead – (again I refer to the Book of Revelations), and onward to each Deity in the hierarchy of the divisions and individual planes, but channeling out to give life to each plane. While giving life to each plane, there are also Masters and Jivatmas which can pick up this essence of truth out of what is passed out on that plane. Of course this means as it descends it loses much of its force when it has reached this plane, therefore so many of those who must/can reach this truth being passed downward by the first in the hierarchy Sat Purusha, must go up above this plane through the trance state. That is the only way they can get much of the unadulterated truths.

Paul Brunton writes a book, the title (I believe) Message at Arjuna. *Or one similar to this; but anyway he tells how the master sits, rather lies on his couch and the pearls of wisdom fall from his lips, because he is mostly in the trance state. This is the same manner in which Ramakrishna was able to contact the divine wisdom; he stayed most of his life in the trance state. It can be done provided one has another to take care of his body needs to keep it alive, while he is out of it.*

The sooner you learn the fact that God or the Absolute never talks directly to people, but has a way of leading men to the light. There are two methods used by the Supreme One: First, is the method of the whole world, led by Natural Law and personal experience and experimentation – trial and error. The world is going this way for it has not accepted a Master, although different religions proclaim their own God as a master. In this manner knowledge is accumulated by experience but it is hardly useful to the succeeding generation who want to try their own way. The second method is that of following a Master. The Supreme One has designated that only a Master can lead men to the perfected knowledge of God. The plan seems to be that common experience leads the individual up to where he meets a Guru and after that the Guru will give him so much knowledge and experience, gets him into the fifth plane and then he is on his own.

Outside these two methods of dealing with the human race, The Absolute never interferes in the affairs of men. He never speaks to anyone, he is never seen by anyone, nor does he impress anyone's mind. If one gets impressions, or hears a voice, or sees visions, he must understand that the Absolute has nothing to do with it. An individual may be impressed, or spoken to by someone, some inferior deity, angel, or ordinary disembodied Soul, but never the Absolute.

Most of the visions which men have of the greats are mental images. Many persons are misled by claiming they have a Master inside, or on the other side of the veil. No real Master will work this way – it is only after you have had a Master to appear before you and can stand the tests, respond to them properly, then you are to accept him. It is only after you have conquered all barriers, and stand before the Radiant Master on the astral plane called Ashta-dal-Kanwal, can you safely follow him inside yourself. From that point you can talk with him, face to face, as freely as you can talk with anyone outside the body.

Men have talked about God as if he is their next door neighbor. As a matter of fact the less men know about God, the more familiarly they talk of him. However, the most important point to know here is that when anyone enters the higher fields of knowledge, he is able to watch the operation of karma and reincarnation. He can see with a clear vision how it applies to others as well as himself. At this stage he is able to see clearly his own past lives.

Now there are two other ways one can gain the secret knowledge which flows out of the Seat of Knowledge. First, one can get out of his body and travel to the place where a Master might be teaching as in the astral world, or he can go to someone whom he knows in the other worlds and ask questions. The second way, is that he can be given instructions through dreams by a Master, or in a trance state, or when the individual is completely relaxed and in a state between awakening and sleeping. And there is a third way, of course, by practicing the methods of ECKANKAR and picking up the truths as they might come gliding into the mind, by the Audible Sound Current. The latter is a little scanty, but it can be useful when one doesn't make contact with his Master.

Leaving the body is a lost art. It is one of the ways in which one can reach the outer worlds and regain the knowledge which was once his own. When properly trained, one is able to detach himself from the physical body, while still living in that body in perfect health, and travel to all parts of the outlying universe. This is the only true way of making contact with Sat Purusha, the Seat of Knowledge.

More later.

Letters to Gail

June 18, 1963

Dear Gail:

The challenge of aggressive good is that which can overcome the challenge of aggressive evil only! The transformation of greed, lust for power and sensuality – is possible only through spiritual disciplines and the knowledge of God, Jivatma and the other worlds.

It is said in the Bhagavad-Gita that whenever virtue subsides and vice prevails in the lower world, that the spirit of God incarnates itself for the vindication of righteousness and destruction of iniquity. The situation in the beginning of the Gita fits our times, but it also gives a magnificent discourse on the immortality, the non-duality, and the eternity of the Jivatma – that which I am going to give in this letter.

I quote Krishna's words to Arjuna: "Never was there a time when I did not exist, nor you, nor these kings of men. Never will there be a time hereafter when any of us shall cease to be.

"Even as the embodied Self passes, in his body, through the stages of childhood, youth and old age, so does It pass into another body. Calm souls are not bewildered by this.

"Notions of heat and cold, of pain and pleasure, arise, O son of Kunti, only from the contact of the senses with their objects. They come and go; they are impermanent. Endure them, O Bharata!

"That calm man who remains unchanged in pain and pleasure, whom these cannot disturb, alone is able, O greatest of men, to attain immortality.

"The unreal never is. The Real never ceases to be. The conclusion about these two is truly perceived by the seers of Truth.

"That by which all this pervades, know to be imperishable. None can cause the destruction of That which is immutable.

"Only the bodies of which this eternal, imperishable, incomprehensible Self is the indweller, are said to have an end. Fight, therefore O Bharata!

"He who looks on the Self as the slayer, and he who looks on the Self as the slain – neither of these apprehend aright. The Self slays not nor is slain.

"It is never born, nor does It ever die, nor, having once been does It cease to be. Unborn, eternal, permanent, and primeval. It is not slain when the body is slain.

"He who knows the Self to be indestructible, eternal, unborn and immutable – how can that man, O son of Pritha, slay or cause another to slay?

"Even as a person casts off worn-out clothes and puts on others that are new, so the embodied Self casts off worn-out bodies and enters into others that are new.

"Weapons cut It not; fire burns It not; water wets It not; the wind does not wither It.

"This Self cannot be cut nor burnt nor wetted nor withered. Eternal, all-pervading, unchanging, immovable, the Self is the same forever."

The root cause of a man's grief and delusion is the identification of the Jivatma with the body. Fear of death paralyzes him because he is ignorant of the Jivatma's true nature. The wise perform their duties in the world, cherishing always the knowledge of the Jivatma's deathlessness. The ignorant man regards himself as the body, endowed with a Jivatma. The illuminated sage knows that he is the Jivatma, possessed of a body. There lies all the difference between the materialistic and the spiritual view of life.

Socrates, rightly called the wisest, the noblest, and the most just man of his time, lived, worked and died under the spell of immortality. Cheerfully he died, giving a discourse on the Jivatma's immortal nature. The meat of philosophy which tells that a man can be sustained in his hour of weakness is vividly described in the Book of Job. When that righteous man bemoaned the loss of his property, and death of his children, and when, suffering from an excruciating physical ailment, he longed for death, the Lord told him about the creation, explaining how insignificant a man is as a physical entity, and asked Job to gird up his loins like a real man. However, in the Gita, Krishna explained the meaning of various yogas or spiritual disciplines by means of which a man attains to the highest goal. They are suited to different temperaments. The active mind pursues the discipline of selfless work. The philosophical mind discriminates between the Real and unreal and renounces the unreal. The introspective aspirant practices self-control and analyzes various states of the mind with a view to ascertaining what lies in the inmost depth of consciousness. The emotional person cultivates an all-absorbing love for God and thereby sublimates his lower passions and desires.

The inner controller of man, God, walks through all feet, sees through all eyes, hears through all ears, eats through all mouths, thinks through all minds, etc. By Its own inscrutable power, the Godhead appears as the personal God, the creator, preserver, and destroyer of the universe, man's redeemer, and worshipped as Father-in-Heaven, Jehovah, Allah, etc. He manifests Himself through divine incarnations. God becomes man so that man may become God. And there is the harmony of religions spoken of in the Gita; the different faiths are like so many pearls in a necklace, and God runs through them like the string. God accepts man's worship, without regard to its form, provided it is whole – and sincere. His knowledge is everlasting.

The special message of the Gita is that of Karma-Yoga, the discipline of right activity, by which a man can attain to the highest good. Karma or work covers all actions of man: physical, verbal or mental. No embodied Soul can live without action, even for a moment. A man's survival demands action; inactivity brings stagnation and death. An action can be a fetter or a liberator, depending on the worker's inner attitude. An egocentric action, performed for a selfish purpose, acts as a chain, for it creates attachment to the result and binds the worker to the phenomenal world, while at the same time if performed in a detached spirit for the whole it acts as a liberator. When the worker works as God's instrument, surrendering to Him the results, good or evil, pleasant or painful, this is the secret of right activity. It is man's lower self that is affected by good and evil and clamors for the results of actions. But there is the Higher Self in man who is the witness and not the doer, the spectator and not the actor. When the Higher Self can rise above the pair of opposites, good and bad, and see the non-action in action, then the secret of right activity is known. All action, if performed in right spirit, enables one to commune with God.

Both contemplation and work are effective spiritual disciplines which will bring most problems under control and give one peace and awareness.

More later.

June 19, 1963

Dear Gail:

The subject is "Beyond God." This is an expression used by many of the Sufi saints in trying to explain that in the original state of the Absolute, or beyond the beginning, there is the state of GOD-IS. In this state IT-IS – unbounded absolute vacuum prevails.

Now I am not getting into anything which can be stretched beyond your imagination, but holding it within bounds. Referring back to the Grand Divisions again, which I gave you in one of the letters, remember I said that within the Second Grand Division the name of God was known as Brahm, and is retained by many Indian saints to designate the ruler of the three worlds, including the physical universe. This is the spiritual-material region, and beyond this is the unbounded void which many cross beyond reaching the Third Grand Division, where God is manifested in a spiritual form far purer than below.

The Second Grand Division is known as the Brahmanda, meaning the Egg of Brahm because it shaped in this manner – of an egg. The upper portion of this world is Par Brahm and ruled over by Maha Kal. The lower region is called Tirkuti, which is the home of the Universal Mind you hear metaphysicians speak of so familiarly. The whole region is divided into countless planes or subdivisions, and in these regions are the heavens of the orthodox religions. I explain a great deal of this thought in The Tiger's Fang. *Here you find God as the Trinity of the Christians – also God the creator-preserver-destroyer of the Hindu religion. It is Brahm, the fountainhead who creates the illusions of the worlds below, as the eternal dreamer.*

The state beyond the Second Grand Division is that which is known to the Sufi as the state of Wara-ul-Wara, or the absolute vacuum. This is that area which must be crossed in order to enter into the heavens in pure spirit. Now in describing this, one speaks of the State of God-Is – describing the state which prevails beyond the beginning of this beginning of creation. This is the world of nothingness which the Buddhists describe and Zoroaster spoke of it; I'm not certain if Christ brought up the subject at all in any of the gospels. However, most orthodox religions that speak of this area appear to think that it is that Ocean of Spriit out of which God manifests life – but it is the most finite creation point of the universes below. This is what might be called the OM point – the most finite point from which the Nothing projects out of Nothingness. This creation point is only that entity or Lord of the Second Grand Division we know as Brahm, who projects the creativity of God through Itself to the worlds below. His power is so great that many upon reaching this plane believe that they have found the heaven which their earthly religion has given them.

It is here that the original cause point is found – that which is called the OM point. This is where the original of the story of Adam and Eve occurred – for they were cast out of this heaven upon the earth where a gross body had to be used, and forever afterwards unhappy for they had left the Garden of Eden involuntarily. Here the word or Lahar is first heard by psychic sense of hearing. This void or world of nothingness is more than what it may sound, for it is a volcanic force of raw atoms which must be shaped into a living stream to become that of the negative nature to serve the worlds beyond. Remember that you do not get out of the negative world until reaching the Third Grand Division.

As I have stated, man or the individual thinks that he has reached heaven upon getting into this region of the universes; and because he hears so much about the void or nothingness which is on the upper level of this world he looks at it with the finality that nothing is there – therefore he cannot leave his world of paradise, and explore that space.

Actually there is the first raw power of the Absolute in this world of nothingness, and it is such a force of pure spiritual force that few entities can go beyond it into the world of the Absolute. Hardly any Jivatma can cross this world of nothing to enter into that far land unless he has a spiritual master to escort him–I speak of this in The Tiger's Fang–*of having to cross the world of darkness. The Void as the Buddhists call it, are little aware of what lies beyond. I once talked with a Buddhist monk who made claims that it is the end of time – the divine state in which God rests as non-consciousness, and appears as consciousness in the first world – the world of Brahm. This was the extent of his knowledge as taught in the monasteries. When I tried to point out that this was only a place where the unending chain of alternating absorption and ejection of consciousness and impressions from out the state of pure spiritual worlds, he would have no part of the argument. He had reached his end of knowledge.*

Actually this is a part of the evolution of the Jivatma, coming out of the realm of the highest world it must make its way down into the physical universe. There is a reason for this action; it is that the Absolute in Its creation of new atoms or Jivatmas, must have use for them – but they have to have a certain amount of experience or tempering like steel which can only be had in the worlds below; they must be tempered by the negative well as the positive. For this reason the Absolute created the lower worlds, and in Its long journey through the areas of time and space, being bound sometimes by the negative power and other times by the positive power, It is being tempered for re-entrance into the heavenly worlds again. It has need for becoming completely pure, for the Absolute needs the pure atom or Jivatma in the running of his creations.

So when the Jivatma returns to the highest heaven again it is a pure Soul, completely tempered and made into usefulness for the Absolute, who can use it intelligently and wisely, and it having intelligence and wisdom now can serve its mission throughout eternity. Consider how many Jivatmas there are throughout all the universes in training for the return to the heavenly heavens; then you can understand what the greatness of the Absoluteness is – and how he uses everything in all his worlds for a purpose.

Now this land of darkness or the void is like a feathery world, and can be shaped according to the power of the Master. He will make it fearful, or a warm comfortable darkness through which he and his disciple can travel. Here one finds the strange humming sounds of the Audible Life Current so much greater than ever heard on the planes below – and for the reason that the Life Current is in storage like a power station for some light company through the city; the deities below are given so much power to pass out into those worlds, and drawing from this void and forming into numerous aspects of life it is like a great river, or a flood of water moving over a landscape, but with that life-giving manna that feeds everything in the worlds below the void. You can see now why the orthodox religionists believe that this is the end of the universe and where God dwells. And you can see why they are so greatly mistaken in this belief!

More later.

Letters to Gail

June 22, 1963

Dear Gail:

At the onset I am handing you an assignment – that is to read 100 books on religions, philosophies, occultism, and similar subjects starting Monday, June 24. I want you to list the names of these books and hand the list to me the day before you leave on your vacation, which is about two weeks. As I have said, this doesn't mean you need to do a complete reading but you can do skipping or scanning.

Take the subjects in this manner: 25 books on religion; 25 books on philosophy; 25 books on occultism; and 25 books on allied subjects (psychology, New Thought, etc.). Start today on this!

Now the subject is "The Seven Fold Veil." The veil is a word used as a symbol of the separation between man and God, under the illusion of cosmic duality. The Masters call it the Veil or the Curtain. Since there are seven of these veils which stand between man and God, they are often discussed in the writings of the masters and disciples. Hafiz, the great Persian poet, once wrote, "Stand aside, you are the covering over Self," and Kabir, referred to the removal of the seven folds of the Veil in this manner, "Open the folds of your veil, and find God."

The Veil that separates an ignorant man from the Absolute Who Is All Knowledge is so subtle that even the highest and finest thought cannot pierce through it. This veil consists of seven folds of seven different, deep colors. Each fold is tied with a separate knot; thus there are seven knots to seven folds. These seven colors represent the seven root desires, corresponding to the seven fundamental impressions, i.e., lust, greed, anger, vanity, attachment, passion, and falseness of life. (See letter on these.) These are connected with the seven openings of sensations in the face, viz. (1) mouth, (2) right nostril, (3) left nostril, (4) right ear, (5) left ear, (6) right eye, (7) left eye.

These veils are actually the root desires in man, and they are the illusions which bind him to the body and to this material reality. When an initiate actually succeeds in actually entering the divine path it is for him a single seven-in-one achievement, and it applies to the first of the seven folds of the veil: (1) the unfastening of the first knot, (2) disappearance of the first fold, (3) crushing out of the first root desires,

(4) wiping out of the relative fundamental impressions, (5) doing away with the first of the seven deep, dark colors, (6) entrance through the door (represented by the mouth) and (7) arriving on the first subtle plane in the other worlds.

In other words the colors are part of the aura, dark in negative nature, and must be dissolved and replaced by the bright colors of pure spirituality. This is the learning of the use of the psychic senses – for by discarding the physical senses and working into the subtle senses one learns how to move in and out of his body, eventually at will. But he must first untie the knots before proceeding any further into the next worlds, and then under the direction of a Master. In getting into the subtle worlds and seeing all the beauty there, he is held spellbound and doesn't generally care what happens, for he often mistakes it for the ultimate reality.

Usually it is only a pure Master who can take the disciple into the other worlds through explorations, and by separating him from the seven fold veils. Should one find a Master who is willing to do this it may be done without effort or problems which normally arise when the disciple tries to make the trip alone.

For your purpose of knowledge, there are seven planes which are spoken of in the four grand divisions – in other words, the first four planes which I speak of are the four grand divisions, plus three planes in the highest. There are no words to describe these worlds so it's only left to your imagination what they might be. This universe is the only universe which has a so-called civilization, and its civilization is nothing but a set of learned attitudes and social habits. Chief among them is the demand men habitually make upon themselves and their associates for mutual respect, dignity with loyalty and social conduct.

In dreams, an ordinary man is able to make partial use of his subtle body with subtle consciousness, but only in respect to gross experience and concerning only gross objects. Just as he experiences the gross world with full gross consciousness through his gross body, so will the neophyte, on the first plane, begin to experience the subtle world with subtle consciousness through his subtle body.

The subtle doors to which the Jivatma may leave the body must be closed, except one, and that is the psychic door of the Third Eye! The Jivatma may leave the body from this point, which is generally the normal way, or he can get out through the psychic door of the thousand petaled lotus–poetic name of top of skull. These doors are the inner sites of the seven Veils I've spoken about – the Veils are the outer symbol of escape and the doors are the inward symbols of escape. All outer senses have a psychic sense, hence the Veil, as it is called. These outer doors or escape hatches must be closed by taking the concentration away from them and placing it on the inner escape points, mainly the Atma – or Third Eye!

This sounds so much like superstition, or hocus-pocus, but any seeker who has gone beyond these Veils knows that a neophyte must not force his way across the border or he will be in trouble. However, once the starter in these sciences learns the secret words, or the passport words which will carry him across the border into the subtle worlds, then he is safe; otherwise his safety lies with a Master guiding him. But he must first be escorted through the gates of the far countries in order to learn the means of travel and learn the passwords.

This Veil is spoken of in "Mystic Experiences of Medieval Saints," by R.P. Aug. Ponlain, S.J., in his part on St. Francis Xavier: "After this prayer, I once found myself inundated with a vivid light; it seemed to me that a veil was lifted up from before my eyes of the spirit, and all the truths of human science, even those that I had not studied, became manifest to me by an infused knowledge. This state of intuition lasted about twenty-four hours, and then, as if the veil had fallen again, I found myself as ignorant as before."

In the Zohar, "the book of splendor," which is the sacred scripture of the Cabbala, it says: "Believe not, says the Zohar, that man consists solely of flesh, skin and veins. The real part of man is his soul, and things just mentioned are only outward coverings. They are only veils, not the real man. When man departs this life, he divests himself of all the veils which cover him."

A Master can strip one of these veils by what is called "The Master's Gaze" or the Twaji – see the letter on this which I sent. All of the teachings go together.

More later.

Letters to Gail

June 23, 1963

Dear Gail:

This is an extension of "Beingness"; however, I'm taking up the space-making side of it. That is that man must make generous room for his fellowman and he hopes that room will be made for him. A lack of space given to an individual, a race, a group can be the result of several things, mainly: tradition, legendry, attitudes, habits, and pridesaving, etc.

When a personality or group is strongly slanted toward conflict so that attention and energy are more often focused by fear and hostility than by confidence and good will, and where the maintenance of pride and security is made to depend upon winning and dominating, disaster lies ahead. Such a personality or group will tear down what it cannot rebuild; and as the tensions of conflict become the very conditions of its being, it will progressively deny itself the types of growth by which it might save itself. Thus, if allowed to be itself or to make space for itself, those factors may dissolve of their own accord.

If we want others to think broadly and feel deeply in our presence then I must give them room to do so. They must be provided with space enough to hold the sort of thoughts and feelings I ask them to have. If, for example, I want them to consider all sides of a subject, I must give them the mental chance to walk around it and look at it from all sides. It makes no sense for us to argue them into a corner where they think only how to hold their own against me or how to escape. If I want them to be people of vision, it makes no sense for me to suspend over them, like the Sword of Damocles, my own viewpoint – letting them know that they had better see things as I see them, or else.

Before one yields to the impulse to put another person on the spot, bludgeon him into compliance, or trap him into making a fool of himself, I must decide what kind of person I want him to become: what marshalling of energies I hope to encourage. You must remember that not many people will give you space – they will put you on the defensive by a remark. It takes a generously structured self to make for another person the kind of psychic space in which he can find room for his self-respect and the acknowledgement of his emotional problems and limitations.

Making psychic space for another means, among other things, making room for thoughts and feelings that may not be pretty, brave or noble, but for making him broader and greater and deeper. Sometimes by admitting a self-mistake one gives another psychic space. By admitting fear where it is the case to be frightened gives space to others. People need room to recognize and acknowledge their less praiseworthy thoughts and emotions so that they can manage them while they are still manageable; but even more, perhaps, people need room to turn around when they find themselves going in the wrong direction. They need psychic space in which to correct errors – and move beyond them.

Since man is a mistake-maker, he is bound to his body through these mistakes – but once he is given acknowledgement that his mistakes are not as stupid as he thought, he is given space in which he is freed. He is also an ego-defending animal, for when he makes a mistake and is taunted, punished, etc., he withdraws his space, but if overlooked he makes psychic space and rectifies his mistakes.

I'll say that 90% of us humans will certainly develop tactics of self-defense that are tactics of self-deception and self-distortion when cast in the role of a fool, etc. We learn to disown our errors and excuse them, and by the way of compensation, we'll become hypercritical of others. We don't admire those who never admit mistakes, who time and again drag up old errors as a basis for new reproaches. Usually we dodge where our own mistakes are concerned and make it hard for other people to admit theirs. Instead of giving them room to turn around and supportive companionship while they make the turn, we edge them into a corner – where as trapped creatures try to defend themselves.

Now this is what I've been calling traps – psychic traps. If you squeeze the space on others, or let your own space be squeezed in by someone, you are falling into a trap. No space – all trap! See? But psychic space is not something we can make for others if we can't make it for ourselves. You must be able to translate all experience that you have and have not been able to handle into a positive, frank, but imaginative outlook on life.

There are two kinds of neurotics who can't handle space. First, is the victim of self-pity, who lives in a world where people do not understand or appreciate him and circumstances are against him. He hates the world and resists any experience which will make it appear less hateful for his derogatory description of the world is his chief justification for his own inadequate conduct of life. The more convincing it becomes in reality the more panic-stricken is his rejection of the world. The second type of self-trapped neurotic is the hostile type. He holds within himself the anger from past defeats, so unresolved and so inclusive that it attaches, constantly, aspects of its likeness. His hostility has several expressions: hypercriticalness, readiness to belittle and disparage; habit of nagging; holds grudges; prejudices, cynicism, suspicion of others' motives; brings all conversations around to alarm or deplorement; takes offense quickly and sees public figures as personal enemies; exploits, humiliates, intimidates, defines success in terms of status and power over others; contempt for soft enterprises of reconciliation. He wants to corner before being cornered, and cannot give anybody room for space.

Some forms of self-trapping are: By trimming our words and attitudes to believing derogatory things about others to the presumed dimensions of other people's understanding. Second, accepting a success goal which is far too small for ourselves. Third, narrowing the mind or closing it on another whose way of life depends for its integrity upon the mind remaining open.

Free men set themselves free. The practice of self-forgiveness is the way to set one's self free. Another way is gratitude – this is an emotion that no one feels or can feel until he has grown into it; and the emotions we arouse in a person – particularly a small child when one demands that he feel gratitude – are the very ones most likely to prevent his growing into it. By nagging or being angry with a child only causes him to have an in-turning attention and makes him feel inadequate; when a gratitude is given to the child it creates an out-turning attention, which is natural. Gratitude can never be felt and never is felt except by those who have grown up enough to feel the reality of others.

The maker of psychic space not only releases people from entrapment, but releases them into a sense of actual roominess. He invites them to growth, and this growth is that which brings greater awareness, and this is what the Jivatma is seeking.

More later.

Letters to Gail

June 24, 1963

Dear Gail:

The subject is "spiritual problems." There are a number of problems which you must look for in the spiritual journey, and which can be overcome provided one takes the right approach to them. They are hardly unusual in their nature, but generally are those which one must face during his travels in seeking knowledge elsewhere.

We are fortunate to have ancestors who found answers to the spiritual problems posed for man. They are: Socrates, Plato, Aristotle, Euripides, Zeno the Stoic, Euclid, Thucydides, Abraham, Moses, Isaiah, Hosea, Micah, David, Matthew, Mark, Luke, John, Paul, Confucius, Lao-Tse, Zoroaster, Gautama, Mohammed, St. Francis, St. Teresa, Thomas Aquinas, Copernicus, Galileo, Newton, Erasmus, Darwin, John Stuart Mill, Jefferson, and hundreds of others. These can be called the champions of liberators of the mind and spirit of mankind.

Among the problems of spirituality are: (1) The Existence of God; (2) The appearance of a Guru for the seeker; (3) From whence came evil if we didn't get it from God the good? (4) How much effect does Karma work in the minute acts of man; (5) Who is to tell one exactly what the will of God might be? (6) How can the mind conceive the desire for a good thing to be an evil in and of itself? (7) How does one die daily and yet live; (8) The way idealism affects the drive of the spirit; (9) The nature of spiritual energies; (10) How does priori knowledge exist as spiritual knowledge; (11) The limitations of knowledge, and (12) The limitations of the spiritual force (positive) in the lower worlds.

These are not quite as major as the problem in which the seeker finds himself upon entering the path to the Absolute. It seems that all hell breaks loose, and this is the great puzzle for everybody who thinks the pathway of God should be easy, and without the problems which do exist. It makes one think that Satan has let loose his demons to torment and bring his former follower back into his fold. The medieval saints and mystics believed they were fighting Satan and his demons in hell, and in a sense they were. But what they were really battling was the reactive mind, the engram and the aberration which must be overcome before one can rise higher on the path of the spiritual. This isn't easy –

but you will have trouble provided you try to make sense with a clergyman or a religionist for they have one stock answer: "We must suffer in this life," or "The Will of God is mysterious," and another is "God knows what to do."

What this amounts to is a matter of depth psychology, yet it is the first step on the spiritual path. The seeker can get rid of these engrams, aberrations (see letters on reactive mind and depth psychology) but it must be done by someone who knows the art of breaking him free from these problems, or through a professional in the field of psychology. An aberration or engram can be centuries old in the individual's mind, or Jivatma – and if the latter, it is harder to erase than mind problems. But some masters undertake the relieving of these tensions. Somewhere in my notes I have a discourse on this spiritual problem.

So many times the individual will panic when this starts happening to him, but there is nothing to be frightened about. Whatever problem it is, it is going to come to the forefront and be with the individual in sharp contrast to what it was previously. The reason being that the more the Jivatma becomes purified, the tougher it becomes for the individual to live with the outer world. He sees and thinks in clearer light, he sees life in a completely new light, and for a period cannot understand why mankind pursues its destructive path. If the individual has a temper, then his anger becomes more apparent until he realizes that it is holding him back, so his second problem now becomes Self-Control. And here I come back to the major basic problem of all spiritual problems which is DESIRE!

One must separate himself from desire, and have an attitude of non-attachment. Buddha explained very patiently to his own followers that desire was the cause of all pain. So you see if you are desiring something, you are attached to that desire, and I can safely say that you'll never have it. (Look at the article on Yang and Yin). But when you are willing to give up your desire and attachment on that object, it most likely will pursue you instead of you pursuing it. Whenever one fails to oppose any attack upon himself he is usually freed of the assault. I am saying all this again, in a different way from what has been written you previously – but it is important for this is the major problem of the traveler on the path.

A good example of this is the story of St. Anthony of the Desert, who fought the good fight nightly against the Demons. It would do you well to get the biography of this master-saint in the library for reading on this point. What he was fighting were his own illusions, arising out of his engrams: that which was appearing in his universe. Example, the other night I had a vision of the world splitting down the center, but realized it was of my own making in my own universe; for a moment it was frightening. But had I not known, it could have driven me off into the deep end. This is what most saints, travelers on the path, mystics, etc., are struggling against only they feel that God is tempting them, or the Devil is working to frighten them back into accepting his rule. In a sense the latter is true for since we live in a negative universe, under the rule of Kal Niranjan (Kal meaning negative and Niranjan the ruler of this universe) we are subjected to the negative forces and maya or illusionary forms which might appear at anytime. This force doesn't want its peoples to leave its world and go into the spiritual and will fight against this, but if one is persistent he can force his way through this.

This is why Love is the basic element taught to the followers of the spiritual path. It is the safest way for the traveler to follow. He is not apt to get into trouble by scrapping with anything physical or invisible should he practice the art of non-resistance, love or good-will toward all things, including himself. Naturally self-forgiveness enters into this and if one doesn't practice self-discipline then he cannot move very far along the path. If one errs he cannot accept guilt; for if he is guilty then he must practice self-forgiveness, but he must be really self-forgiving and not be shifting blame. I remember an old editor who said this to me when I'd made enough mistakes for the day. "Your mistakes were made today. Tomorrow we start a new day, and if there are mistakes they will be new mistakes."

I am going to take up the various problems of spirituality which were named earlier and discuss them with whatever space is felt necessary to do so. Some will be a full letter and others much shorter in space. Most of them are the general problems which are always in front of whoever enters on the path of the spiritual goal. The yardstick can be applied against the behavior of others as well as against yourself. Be kind to yourself in applying it, yet be merciless in standing off and taking a good look. But above all, please do not be too analytical of yourself, for this is the easiest way to fall into the trap of maya.

More later.

Letters to Gail

June 26, 1963

Dear Gail:

I take up the "Existence of God," which is the first problem which any disciple meets with upon entering the path. Not a unique problem, but one in which all people sooner or later encounter provided they at least have a thought about the Absolute.

The existence of God is always a moot question. It is this point that orthodox religions make that one must have faith. Perhaps five persons out of every thousand might have an experience which proves to them the existence of something beyond their powers of comprehension, but there is hardly anything to sustain the other 995 for faith in a Creator except what they are told by the priest and the sacred writings. Therefore, within the writings of every sacred literature, the first thing to be considered is that of faith, and the seeker is told that if he cannot believe the teacher or the priest there is little that can be done for him.

This is certainly true, in a sense of speaking; however, since the average teacher or priest cannot reveal to the disciple the existence of God, the impatient and the God-hungry seeker makes his demand for the proper revelation. If it is not forthcoming then he goes elsewhere for the understanding that there is such a thing as the Divine It – and that nothing is more proven to him than the revelation which is given him.

Therefore one must accept the attitude as that in the past. The existence of God IS. Therefore, the seeker has already received, or he has to establish himself as living in the present – in the ISNESS of God – In the Now! He cannot live in any other attitude. One of the strange experiences which I had in this manner of speaking was when I made up my mind to have an experience with God at a particular hour, on a particular day of the week. Thereafter, all my thoughts, all my mind were concentrated upon this hour, when I was to experience the existence of God. I grew more nervous as the hour approached, and when it arrived, I was at exhaustion point from worry, fatigue and my nerves shot; but nothing happened. I felt relieved at this, and went into the bedroom, laid down and relaxed; suddenly the experience came while I was in a half-coma, between awakening and sleep.

The perplexing question posed before every individual is, "Is there a

God?" If so, who or what is IT? Where and how may he be contacted, and what has IT for mankind. Now the question is not WHO, WHERE and HOW. But it remains that the question is put to one in the form of an adverb – WHY? The philosophers of all schools agree that the first three questions are right, but none agree upon the reason of God. This is the ultimate answer to the Existence of God. Unless one knows this answer, he cannot know the other questions and answers to them, concerning the Existence of the IT.

The answers to the WHY of God is in the ISNESS of God! Since IT IS then the existence is there. The ISNESS is concerned with the Beginning and the Ending of creation, and since God is concerned with the circle, instead of the Alpha and Omega he is therefore always standing in the line of the circle, as the IS of All! ALL IS, in other words, contains the fullness of ALL Eternity! Remember the letter on the Four Conditions of Life?

To be dialetical about the Absolute seems to be only making words. But it leaves a curious query – did God create man, or did man create God? Since both logic and history are unreliable then one must look at something other than these two subjective qualities of man; logic is the law of thought as recorded in this universe, and history is the record of the reactive mind of man, or the record of his aberrated behavior. I personally become terribly fatigued with reading the records of individuals or the records as given by history. What does it amount to – hardly more than the misbehavior of individuals who changed the course of certain directions in which mankind is headed.

God exists as the formless! This is the secret of Himself, or the ISness of that which we call God! Being the formless, man never sees IT! Nor could man or Jivatma see the Absolute IT if he entered into the highest heaven where the Divine Absolute lives. Kabir said, "God is the breath of all breath!" This is the finality of the true existence of God. Yet how can I prove the existence of God, for it is a personal experience. When you see the living form of trees, animals, or the running water in a brook, this is not God in existence, for it is the essence of what He Is! This sounds paradoxical, but it is true for God is not the lower spirit which makes up matter and acts as the forming power. That is a part of his nature, but not God Itself, e.g., the body is not me, but a part of the nature which makes up this self, but the true self is that hidden part in me called the Jivatma. Then think of God as the same; for he is not all the things which so many religionists and metaphysicians claim. The beauty of this world, the sunset, the mountains, lakes, oceans, and parts of nature are not God, but the things which He created out of his lower nature, just as you or I would take the necessary ingredients and bake a cake.

Poets sing of these parts of nature being God, but this isn't true. There is a school of philosophers called the natural philosophy – which is only a study of the physical universe and its laws, and that man could live better in this state – primitive state of nature than in the present civilization. In order to make contact with God, the Absolute, the Jivatma must rise above this universe into the other worlds, until he passes through the world of Brahm, through the Veil or the dark Void into Sat Desha. This is when one begins to learn of the existence of God, the Whyness of IT!

It always seems to me that the orthodox religions were sterile in their teachings and looking back on my days spent in India, I've come to think the same of those teachings. If life consists of a series of births, life, and death, without seeing the existence of a major power, then I cannot have any part of it, and yet how would I get out of this life? This query has the loaded power of a proof of the existence of something which is existence to prove that LIFE is greater underneath than what we can observe outwardly. The query has proof that the existence of an Absolute is greater than our imagination, and herein lies the pudding with its evidence. The subsistence of Kabir's statement brings home the point. "God is the breath of all breath!" With the essence of the atom chain in the space of the universe, one can understand the presence of some Deity shaping them into various forms, which gives beauty to the physical senses of the human – but not being a part of them Itself.

This shaping of things forms another part of the WHYNESS, for it is the As-is-ness of life, or the existence of God. The existence of the great Entity only proves that He is there, but not in it. The creation of a thing and the destruction of a thing, at the moment of either part, is the As-is-ness of IT. The Alter is-ness is the survival between these two points and makes for the Whyness or the existence of God.

More later.

Letters to Gail

June 28, 1963

Dear Gail:

The second problem named in the letter on spiritual problems is "Where to find the Guru." This is an important lesson in any case for the search to find the Guru might continue for a lifetime. Very often it does just that.

Once when Peter Openisky (I'm not certain if this is the way his name is spelled) was in search of a Guru, he wrote a friend in India that he was coming to that country to seek a religious teacher. Several days after the Indian friend got the letter, an old man appeared at the door stating that he was PO's Guru, and that he wanted to stay there as a servant to wait on PO to see if he would be recognized. PO came to visit his friend, stayed for several months, looked for a Guru, and never found one, although the real Guru was acting as his servant, but not recognized. PO went back to England disappointed, to make a public statement that there were no spiritual teachers in India as so claimed by the thousands.

It is said that when the student is ready the teacher appears. I can vouch for this statement. Each time I've been ready to make another upward step, a teacher designated for teaching on that particular level appeared in some manner or other. I've found this always to be true, and never worried about learning what would be on the next higher level of the spiritual worlds. There are specialists in spiritual matters on the far side of the curtain well as on this side. These specialists are always saints, and in a manner of speaking all Gurus are saints, but all saints are not Gurus. A Sat Guru is a saint who has been appointed by the Supreme Sat Nam, ruler of the first plane of the fourth grand (the highest) division, sometimes known as the fifth plane. The Guru is sort of a viceroy, or an executive officer who does his work on this plane. The Sat Guru who is the highest type of Guru (Sat means true and Guru, light-giver) is the chief instrument of the meaning true, and leader of the people into spirituality, and is the main channel of the Supreme Ruler to contact this world of humanity.

Most Sat Gurus have received their appointment from the Highest Ruler, and they only are capable of performing the duties of giving the initiation, and of leading their disciples to the home in Sach Khand. He is sort of executive officer for the Absolute. Three terms are always used in the matter of masters. They are: Master, Sat Guru and Saint, but they mean the same in all religions. When the Christians speak of a saint, they are speaking of a master and a sat guru synonymously. But it isn't the canonical saint of the church. Such saints are made saints by decree of the pope and his church, while the real saints develop into saints by their own hard work under the directions of their Gurus and by their help. There is no other way to become a real saint.

A genuine master is the super-man of history, and by virtue of his development, he has become the prototype of the race, the most splendid specimen of manhood, the noblest of the noble. He has the best of health, a high, keen, penetrating mind, quick of wit and sound of judgment. He may not be educated by formal education, but his mind has undergone the hardest training and discipline. He is the only man ever manifested in all history in whom individualism and universalism are combined in their full expression; this in spite of the assertion of some philosophers that such a combination is impossible. But you see the Master stands alone, for he is a law unto himself, does what he pleases, and he asks favors of no man.

Neither can any man hinder him in the execution of his will, for he has all things at his own command, and if he suffers hardships, or inconveniences, that is because he chooses to do so for some purpose. He is the supreme giver, not a receiver and he always pays for what he gets. He is slave to no one, is no time server, is bound by no rule or custom outside of himself, and he is a citizen of the whole world. His life and teachings are universal. He belongs to no race or time, but to all nations and all times. He is a paradox in religion, teaches no theology, has none, yet he is the most religious of all. His system is not a religion, yet it leads to the most complete religious experience, and the happiest, for he is absolutely universal in all his teachings. He has no creed, yet he never antagonizes any creed, sect, or institution. He finds no fault with anyone or anything, yet he draws the sharpest lines between the good and bad. He considers human weakness only an illness brought on by aberrations or engrams.

If you are looking for a master, how would you go about finding one? This question is asked by all seekers. First, you look for the perfect man – I mean, one who has a perfect character. Secondly, listen to the inner voice, or the voice of intuition. The voice usually tells if your feeling is correct. Thirdly, I know that once you see the Master in his radiant form, you have found him, and need look any further. Fourth, if you are seeking a master, you must realize that he is seeking you, rather approaching you, and it is only a question of time when this great event will come about. For the old saying goes, "When the chela (student) is ready, the Guru appears!"

The ECK Masters never boast of their mastership, or of their spiritual powers, or attainment. Masters never complain of their treatment at the hands of others. Masters never find fault or blame others. Masters never punish anybody, but leave the punishment to the negative power whose business is to administer justice. Their lives are governed entirely by the Law of Love. Masters hardly give to ascetic practices or unreasonable austerities. Masters never beg for a living. Masters never perform miracles for public exhibitions. It is a fixed law that real saints never do miracles to win disciples. A genuine master teaches and practices the Audible Life Stream, or Sound Current, called the Shabda.

If one is prepared to find the master, he will appear. But a master will never appear to be a master, if one is not prepared. He can be your next door neighbor, make talks to people, and give them spiritual help, but many if told he is a master, would never believe it. Yet only a few can recognize his spiritual status. Those who cannot see the Master, because of self-blindness, die in spiritual poverty, when only the opening of their eyes would give them the vast riches of a new life. No one can discover a master when blinded by their own pre-conceived notions. IN OTHER WORDS NO ONE CAN DISCOVER THE MASTER UNTIL CERTAIN INNER PREPARATIONS HAVE BEEN MADE. This is the whole secret of the mystery of finding a master; you must be prepared in the inner-self, then he is able to step forth and see the master.

These letters in a sense are serving that purpose, not to prepare you, but to show you how to prepare yourself so that when you are ready, the spiritual blindness falls from your eyes and you see the Master in his radiant form – and then you no longer will have doubt of yourself and the direction in which you are traveling.

More later.

Letters to Gail

June 29, 1963

Dear Gail:

Whenever one can say that this is the answer to an abstract question, then the form is set-in and the subject becomes rigid and forms an orthodoxy. When Christianity says that it is the way and the only way, this is the time to withdraw from the sect; when Buddhism says it has the only way, then it's time to leave, and this goes with every religion. What I'm trying to say here is simply this: One must leave room for further searching, always! When the goal is won, when the victory is had, there must be something further or the Jivatma goes down! I mean down the spiral to something lower than what he was before, and must make the climb upward again!

Anyway the third subject is "From Whence Came Evil If We Didn't Get It From God, the Good?" A moot question indeed! So in order to understand what is called evil one must go back to the letters on the spiritual divisions, and planes, and The Tiger's Fang. *It concerns the lower planes which are under the Kal forces (Kal means negative force). All up to the Brahm plane are under the Kal forces – in fact, Brahm is the God of Negative forces. The Christian God, Buddhist God, and any orthodox God; all are entities of this plane, the highest god which mankind knows through his religion. This is why the Masters are necessary, they have reached the pinnacle of religious success. Though I admire and praise the Christian Saints for their struggle to achieve the glory of the Absolute, I am not sure that any did – I say that, I'm not certain: I say this because their lives as recorded do not bear out the fact that they did! Certainly they have achieved so much more than I have, and should I have at least a 16th of the degree of spirituality as St. Francis it would give great happiness. But my ambition is to be closer to God than what I know he was.*

The whole record of the individual man, as we know through history, biography, autobiography, and other documents is that of struggle against the Kal force; and a large number of them in an effort to gain the spiritual force or the positive force of God. This record if you have read enough is a sorrowful affair of the individual lost in the mire of grief, apathy, anger, and other emotions on the lower tone scale. But it appears that this is a struggle which one must undertake provided he is to get out of this lower existence into the higher worlds. So this calls for the explanation of what I know about the Existence of Evil, and where it came from. First, you must remember that the Negative Power is but a subordinate to the Supreme One and he rules over the regions of mind and matter, representing the darker side of creation. This doesn't mean that he is altogether bad; but in the very nature of things, what we call as evil exists as the negativity.

The philosophy of evil is: Evil exists only as a shadow. It is the maya of God, on the lower planes, under the rule of Kal Niranjan, so we must assume the thought that if evil exists it is because God allows it. Hence the answer to the question – evil is established by God whether it is directly or indirectly. I would rather judge that it is put here for the purpose to drive the Jivatma into accepting God as the last resort – driven to the wall by the factor of evil without escape, one can make the escape through God, if he will accept the fact that God is the light, and where there is light, how can there be darkness? From the point of view of the Absolute there is no evil, for he sees the karma of man working out the way it has to be.

Kal Niranjan is the supreme God over the negative plane, that which is the negative pole of creation. He has many subordinates and agents. His office is in the Brahm world, located in the plane called Tirkuti, or Brahm Lok, commonly called by orthodox religions as the summit of the Three Worlds or heaven itself. The law is with him; the law of known justice; retribution; and Karma and Reincarnation. He has no power except to obey the will of God, in carrying out the law on the lower grand divisions.

The lower grand divisions operate upon a modus operandi that law is all. This is why we have so much emphasis upon the LAW in this universe, even church laws, man-made laws and other types of laws. So we must as the Jivatma deal with the negative power while in this world; with him we must contend in our struggles for spiritual freedom. It is his duty to try to hold us here, while it is our duty to escape. The resulting struggle purges us and makes us strong, fitting us for the journey to the true home. The struggle, pain and suffering makes us stronger, heartier and ready for the ascent. At the present we are sojourners in this negative world, and it is only through our ignorance or stubbornness which keeps us at this point. Once we learn to work in harmony with the powers above us, we start receiving help and will eventually rise to the position where one finds a master and be accompanied into the higher worlds.

The famed trinity is in this world, Father, Son and Holy Ghost; or Brahma, Vishnu, and Shiva. Here is also the famous Law of Mind over Matter, a law which is only for the lower world of mind, and is so much displayed in PSI now under the study of Dr. Joseph Rhine at Duke University. So you see how little man has advanced since early times, when he was in touch with the higher powers, but let himself drop down into the lower worlds because of this interest in the hedonistic principle rather than that of spirituality. The laws of the negative power are known to man as the "laws of nature." All of which were created by Kal Niranjan. So man's fight is to resist the webs of illusion and see through all into the beyond where dwells the better, the good and the higher things of all life.

Saints pick up the desolate Jivatmas, hungry and weary, and by the aid of Shabda they deliver them from earth bondage and take them into the higher worlds. This constitutes the essential difference between the works of the real masters, and the agents of the negative power. This is why the figure or image of the devil came into existence – since he is supposedly out to capture Jivatmas to keep his kingdom supplied, and it looks pretty full at the time; always has been. But why in God's name does he spend the time with a single individual and not millions? I never understood this argument. So you can now understand why this is a warring universe and can never be anything otherwise, for one day, maybe billions of years from now, or next week – I don't know – this universe will be destroyed, and all Jivatmas will be pulled upward into the next plane, kept there for a thousand years or more and put back on earth again. This has occurred throughout the history of this universe, and nobody can prevent this except God Himself, the very one who orders it.

Evil then is illusion, because it is darkness, and how can one be in darkness if there is light? This is the paradox of evil. Once you have caught the key to this paradox, the explanation of why God allows evil to exist, and why he let it be created in the beginning. Since he created both the positive and negative poles so man could have a grasp of the vastness of spirituality, He remains the Lonely One of all worlds, all universes, and all things. There is no way of explaining who He is, what He is and above all, explaining Him as the creator, of both good and evil, except the way I have – that is, I have no other way.

More later.

Letters to Gail

June 30, 1963

Dear Gail:

The fourth subject is "How Much Effect Does Karma Work In the Minute Acts Of Man?" A subject which must always be included in the study of spiritual problems, and which could easily be answered in a sentence. The sentence being: "Karma is always at work, in every thought and action of the individual while in those planes below the Second Grand Division." However, there must be some explanation of this statement.

Again I repeat as in my last letter the history of man is a study of his fight against the negative forces which must strive to hold him in the physical universe. Karma therefore is the law of the universe, and it must operate according to what its modus operandi is – and according to what the God Kal Niranjan has established for it to work in the lives of man. No man, regardless of his status, except the great masters, is free of the Law of Karma; it works in every act of mind, body and Jivatma – this is the Law, and all other laws are modeled upon it. Our Courts of Justice are based upon this law, the Law of Moses is based upon it, as well as the Code of Hammurabi, the Ten Commandments, the Moral Code, the Protestant Ethical Code, the Constitution of United States and the Declaration of Independence, and of course, The Bill of Rights, Rights of Man, etc., including all the laws of man, and the major law of the East called the Law of Manu. I finally got most of them down.

When man works upon the theory that man-made punishment is illegal then he is working toward the proper goal, for it is not man's place to punish criminals in the sense of capital punishment, as the Law of Karma will take care of any crime. I'm not selling the idea openly that no man should split his neighbor's head, or covet his wife, for all the laws of morality take care of these questions. But what is going to be the punishment of such crimes according to man-made law? This is not an easy answer, and to draw a flat reply is lacking an open mind, for how is one to handle criminals, is something I'm not trained to give answers. But from the overall view of what has gone on in the past I believe that we as a race are certainly giving more study to handling the problems of the criminals and insane.

Unless you trained yourself to see the Law of Karma working out in the individual, nation, race and world, it is hard to understand problems which might be otherwise simple to see and know. So many times I'm lost in my own feelings, prejudices and attitudes that my mind doesn't open wide enough to see the universality of Karma. But once you take an objective view of the situation it is easy to get an insight on how Karma is working through the life of the individual. Last night in the movie I was taking an objective view of "Hud" and his family – how that the situation created in their lives had drawn them together; it was a case of pure Karma that each in his way had lived a life of violence and got themselves together in this particular life. Alma had a violent past; Grandpa had lived a hard, but violent frontier life, Lun was living on the edge of violence, but Hud was the force which tied them all together with his uncontrolled energies. The dead father and mother (Lun's parents) had also figured in the story, both resulting from acts of violence. You see part of the Law of Karma is this: Whatever is drawn to you is the result of your attitude!

This is a most interesting study of the mind, provided one would want to spend his time in a study of Mind. But this is foolish, for such a study is endless and one would spend years taking classwork under learned professors and doing laboratory work. So the answer is to study God, and all else comes to you. Now I don't mean to say that you start out on a long training or study program for an exhausting study of God, but whatever you wish to know at times is to go into your own laboratory – within yourself and learn.

The one thing which beats the Karmic Law (oh yes, there is no discouragement about having to stay under the law of karma) is the higher law, and that is the Law of Love, and this law is a most peculiar sort of law, not anything like we hear so much about from the half-baked metaphysical theorieson the Law of Love. However, I think that Stella Mann, who is really not a thinker, nor can ever be classed as a hard-hitting metaphysical student, wrote a book (three books in fact) on the Law of Love which is exceedingly good. It is in the public library. Read it sometime.

Even though the puny metaphysical cults are confusing and mixed up, they are doing some good with the teaching of their limited knowledge of this higher law. The Christian faith tries to take credit on the Law of Love by pointing out that Christ was the true savior because he brought to the human race the law which broke the Karmic ties of man. They point out that the old Jewish law was "An Eye for an Eye and a Tooth for a Tooth." The exacting revenge which the Karmic Law always takes, and that Christ came to earth to show there was another way of getting past this Law! True, but so did Buddha, and a number of other saviors including Krishna, as he points out in the Gita!

The Karmic Law is exacting, so in detailed that whatever impression is made in this work is registered by the Jivatma or mind and put away in the file cabinet as a picture. (Remember the letter on facsimiles or pictures?) The reaction to the situation again occurring is a karmic act, or the reaction to the picture brought back into the vision of inner image is also a karmic act – the karmic act is made in two manners, when it occurs and when the Jivatma looks at the file picture again, and this is why we are constantly taking pictures within so that the Jivatma can have them to look at. Now if it didn't while in this universe then it would borrow pictures to look at; this is one reason why movies and TV are so popular – it gives the Jivatma some pictures to look at – even though artificial pixs. When one has a picture which makes him ashamed and to feel guilty, he needs to get rid of that pix; often self-forgivenss causes him to drop it, or maybe he can be processed (psychoanalyzed) so it will be pulled out. But normally the Law of Love will take care of many of his problems.

I paused to point out here that since the emphasis has been put so much upon the Law of Love that politicians, clergymen, parents, and party-poopers are using it for their own convenience, to get others in line, to conform to their wishes, or the laws of society. Example, we are now told to love our black race, etc., not that I object to accepting the black race as a first class citizen, but do not love anyone or anything because somebody else desires it; I give my goodwill to all, but my love is special, and that goes only to those whom I wish to love, for I have not the capacity of a saint to spread universal love to all things, all people. Maybe someday I can learn universal love.

I am not certain if this letter is explanatory on the detailed effects of the Law of Karma, but there is so much you must see between the lines and the readings you must do. Read the book "Many Mansions," by Cerminara. It is a good study of the Karmic Law.

More later.

Letters to Gail

July 1, 1963

Dear Gail:

The subject is the fifth spiritual problem, "Who Is To Tell One What The Will Of God Might Be?" A subject which has baffled so many and yet is so simple. The answer is actually through intuition, but it cannot be a simple answer to most of us if we are not in the position to recognize what is the Will of God, and what is not.

Briefly, I will discuss the lower self so that you can get a better understanding of what you might be following or listening to within, and it may not be right. According to Freud (I think it is best to use his theory at this point about the divisions of the mind) we have three sections of the psyche or mind: superego, ego and id. The superego is that part of the psyche which is the conscience, the traditions, parental influence, carries on vicariously the expectations of man's higher nature, the censorship on morals. The ego is that part of the psyche which is self-assertive, self-preserving tendency, and extrovertive. The id which is the reactive mind, the mass tendency of the lower mind, carnal mind, and the coarse, crude instincts. There is another part of this study called the libido, which is the sexual drive, the energy, motive, force, desire as arising from sex instinct or the primal urge to live.

I name these parts because their urgings can at times mislead a person into thinking that it might be the will of God. Even the gods of the negative, but physical world, can mislead a person; there are so many things which can make him think that the Will of God has brought him into a certain state. The ego is the weakest of the three parts of the psyche because it is pulled both ways, and has to defend itself. The censorship of the superego is always butting in and explaining to the ego that it cannot do certain things; the id is always whispering into the inner ear that it's all right. So the poor ego follows that one which is the strongest. This is why the Catholics want the child baptised at birth, brought up in a parochial school, and trained in the church teachings. They teach the superego, or the censorship, to be the strongest of the triangle including the libido.

The Will of God is seldom concerned with the conduct of the individual. That is, the Superego or the Id which takes charge. If someone tells you that it is the Will of God that he takes charge of your life, he is, if sincere, only speaking from the viewpoint of the Id, seldom from the higher planes. This of course is the voice of the negative gods, and one that nobody can have too much interest. So this brings one back to what is the Will of God? The Will of God is that which is Shabda – that which is the Bani, the Word, the Voice of God. This Will is concerned only with the Jivatma and nothing else in man. The action of the intelligent will is a downward orientation towards that of the sense world, or it may take its upward orientation toward a settled peace and equality. When the Jivatma listens to the Audible Life Current, It turns upward, toward the highest heaven. Once the Will of God takes hold, there is no turning back; one must go ahead with his plans to get to the Absolute in those other worlds.

The Master's Will is really the Will of God, for when a disciple is taken as a student, he must follow out the Will of the Master, because the Will of the Highest One is so subtle and invisible that it's not likely that it will be noticed. Therefore the Will of the Master must take over and guide the individual to the proper goals.

The surrender to a Master is not the giving up of all those things which one expects; it is not like the ascetic ways of St. Francis, or many of the orders today throughout the world which practice austerities. The path is hard, but it is not without rewards; those perversions of the mind must go, and whatever might be holding the individual back from rising higher in the other worlds. It is hard enough to rid one's self of what must go, instead of voluntarily fasting, giving up for the sake of austerities. The Master will never seem to be unduly hard, but he will apparently create incidents, or events which will make you face that problem which is deeply bothering you. And you will face the problem, work it out under his watchful eye, hard as it might appear to be – but you can understand that it will never again bother you.

So many assume that the commands of the law-giver is the Will of God. The priests, the prophets and the kings all claim to know the Will of God as their own; but when we challenge their credentials to speak for God, they call us bad names. Ask them any questions of the right and wrong actions, they can never give the fundamental answer. Whatever hinders or delays the Jivatma in Its progress toward spiritual freedom is wrong. Whatever creates bad karma is wrong, and whatever creates good karma is right. Therefore you can say that whatever helps the

Jivatma in Its progress toward spiritual freedom is the Will of God. Whatever creates good Karma is the Will of God.

In the letter on Dharma, I explained this meant righteousness, doing right, obeying the Law of God, and this means doing "what is to be done." This is the Will of God. But hardly no one except the Masters can attempt to tell what the substance of obedience to the Will of God might be. Danda, or the law which sets forth the concrete Will of God, is that foundation and support of all good societies. It is the cornerstone, the pillar of the state, but it is an old trick of priests and politicians to teach the mob that whatever they give out is the "will of God." But Danda serves the Will of God by restraining the evil tendencies of men, protecting the weak, and to some extent developing the higher impulses by inculcating higher ideals. It helps the well disposed people to establish a whole swadharma, the self-imposed discipline.

When one gives himself to the Guru, he will receive the Guru. There is an old Sufi saying, "Give us all you have, and we will give you all we possess." If the disciple gives up all, mind, body, wealth and Soul, to the Master, the Master will in return give the disciple such wealth as no king ever possessed. The divine paradox is – by surrendering all to the Guru, you gain your liberty, for it is only the man who is free who does always the Will of the Master. It is the Will of the Guru, which is the Will of the Supreme One, because the Guru is the representative of the Supreme, by following him, one in turn follows God.

By doing or acting in the name of the Master, one acts in the name of God, and hence he is doing the Will of God. Sounds paradoxical, but one must realize that as an earth-bound Jivatma he cannot reach up to God, so he must find a representative of the Absolute and put himself under the Guru. Otherwise he will blunder, slip and slide through a number of lives until perhaps a Guru will come along and feeling sorry take him under his wing, show him the pathway to heaven by the Audible Life Stream. This is the Will of God, this Life Stream, and one only needs to follow it to know he is rightly following out the Divine Will.

More later.

Letters to Gail

July 2, 1963

Dear Gail:

This is the discussion of the sixth problem which the neophyte must face, "How Can The Mind Conceive The Desire for a Good Thing To Be An Evil In And Of Itself?" When one steps out upon the path he hears so much about humility and humbleness, never about the universal viewpoint, nor of the cosmic consciousness. He is told that he is going to lose his ego, must be rid of this evil and accept the viewpoint of God, and that he is going to dwell in happiness throughout eternity. Such vague goals are ones I cannot conceive. Now this is what I want to point out at this stage of the letters – in the last one I spoke of Freud's theory on Superego, Ego and Id. The Ego represents the self which has contact with the outer world, and uses reason and logic as laid down by the theologians and psychologists, economics, politics, etc., in our lives, say civilization.

The eastern religions are great on saying that we must get rid of the ego; westerners don't pay much attention to this and as a consequence what do they do? They strive to build the ego, filling it with pride and looking to achievements in the outer world. Who is right? Neither one has the right answer, for if one starts out to get rid of the ego then he certainly would have a hard time, and if he starts building up the ego for self-preservation, then he would certainly need a terrible amount of self-confidence in face of what the superego is there for, to censor him, and give him a built-in set of guilt patterns. The id is always trying to get control and let itself manage the body in an unruly way which is opposing the set of social laws in our society.

So we must do something about the ego. First we must learn to set aside the ego whenever we wish. This is part of our training under a master – and we must see that it can be withdrawn when necessary, and put forward for a survival unit when needed. Incidentally its survival means body survival, not survival of the Jivatma. When the mind reaches a point that it considers the desire for a good thing to be an evil in and of itself, there is time to take stock of what is occurring within the mind. Only the Jivatma can do this for it must take the universal viewpoint in looking at itself. Remember this rule, "When the Jivatma looks at itself there is a problem existing, the problem will disappear provided it is duplicated." I probably confused you on this. I only mean to say that a duplication of the original facsimile put together with the original will make it disappear. That's all.

The mind often looks at a good thing, and decides that it is an Evil in and of itself. Most certainly the mind is not the final entity which can look to God itself – it can never reach the highest planes, for it is dropped at the lower half of the fourth plane. If Danda or the Law of God is used in the rule of a community, the mind would find it hard to accept because there isn't any complications in the procedure of the law. The mind must use vias, or terminal points in order to reach its goal while the Jivatma goes directly to its source without complexes, complications or vias. If a good or a positive action arises, the mind most likely would assume that it is an evil within itself, and by this thinking most likely would bring about an evil in the positive action. An example of this was in the movie "Winter Light." The parson could see nothing in the woman who loved him except that she wanted to possess him. Therefore he started bringing about the negative in the woman, because his attitude was demanding that she be negative! He didn't want it any other way. So she was forced into accepting what he was asking of her, and blended in that direction. This is a very subtle way of how the Law of Nature works. For example, once I had a woman who claimed that I would betray her, and that betrayal came about because she looked at me in that light constantly, speaking of what she had to expect of me, and finally one day I did something which she accepted as betrayal. Hence, I betrayed her – but here I'm trying to point out that the mind law is so subtle that you must look deeply in order to understand. It isn't the question of seeing both sides of the question, but lifting one's self to a level where the cosmic or universal viewpoint can see rightly.

The universal viewpoint goes something like this. If the negative forces trap one Jivatma, all Jivatmas can be trapped; if you can look into the depths of the universal and see one Jivatma struggling to be released from this trap you are affected, and must do something to get his release even if it be prayer. Therefore the universal viewpoint is the overall viewpoint. It's like reading a book, you have the opportunity of seeing what is going on in the story, but the individual characters do not. It's like being God and looking at the world, caring what happens yet not being concerned for it is fiction anyway, and all is going to be well in the end for all things end well!

A few more words on the universal viewpoint. If you will notice while reading the newspapers that certain individuals are crusading for certain things. Their viewpoint is narrowed to a limited vision. Businessmen are limited to a narrow vision because they have to concentrate on a profit margin. This is why no field of endeavor will give one the universal viewpoint except the endeavor to reach God. One narrows the point of view to concentrate on God, but once he has received the Light of God, his viewpoint widens into the universal viewpoint. This is what Christ called the "narrow way." Remember his quotation? "A camel can pass through the eye of a needle easier than a rich man can enter into the Kingdom of Heaven." All he was saying is that a man cannot think of materialistic things and of God too. His attention must be on one or the other and since God gives the ultimate why think of the materialistic side of life?

So back to the mind and its insight on evil in good. Since the negative force is in charge on this planet the mind must fight in order to see good in all things, and twist all things for its own advantages. Remember how St. Francis proclaimed all things as his brothers and sisters? He spoke of Brother Winter having come to visit with him; Brother Hunger wanted to stay with him, and he would treat them as his guests. When one meets with adversity then he doesn't take this as adversity but as something good happening, instead of twisting it into an evil, it becomes a positive force. Some people have a knack of using all things as a gainful force in their lives – and this is what keeps them floating on top constantly – you cannot defeat them at all. This is done by a certain attitude which they have developed, that of not allowing the mind to defeat them.

Once you learn how to control the attitude and not allow it to change under any circumstances there will be no spiritual problem of seeing or conceiving the desire for a good thing to be an evil in and of itself. The attitude is not a pantywaist one, but that of strength in dealing with all situations regardless whether they be spiritual or of this world.

More later.

July 4, 1963

Dear Gail:

"How does one die daily and yet live?" This is the seventh spiritual question which one must confront once he steps out on the pathway to the Absolute. The answer is simple if you know Shabda Yoga– that is, you must learn to leave the body at will and dwell on other planes, and return to the body when possible, and at your own command!

In his letters St. Paul used this phrase, "I die daily." This meant that he had control of himself, that he could leave the body at will and come back to it. Therefore he was dying daily and yet he lived! This is the crux and the truth of the whole of life! How then can one bring himself to this point?

He brings himself to this point by first finding the Master as I've pointed out in previous letters concerning the spiritual problems. Then he is initiated and learns how to meet the Master outside the body, and travel the universes of the other worlds. His body is left intact, breathing and with all apparent looks of a live flesh and blood body, but it is only the shell because the spirit has left it and has gone elsewhere! You ask how can the body stay alive when the essentials of its own being has left it; that it has died and yet it will return. Suspended animation is one name of the body when it has suspended all life and can stay in this position until the spirit returns.

Stories are told in India about criminals in the old days who hid themselves in graves while the law searched the countryside in hopes of finding them. They went into suspended animation and left their bodies buried within the graves where nobody would suspect they were hiding. I heard a large number of these stories while in India, though never saw one. I know an Egyptian who does a professional job of getting buried alive and staying underground for at least five days. He has learned the trick of the trance state in which the yogis are adepts at doing, and using it for money-making devices or to sail up to God.

When one wants to go into suspended animation (the trance state) he puts his concentration on the Tisra Til or what is called the Third Eye, and waits for the Master's appearance. If he doesn't have a master, then wait anyway for one will put in his appearance. If you are not certain whether this is a master or not, there are certain code words you may use to determine if you wish to leave your body and go with this entity. These code words are: "In the name of SUGMAD, I order you to give your true identity?" If it is a master, he doesn't worry about such a challenge and will give his true identity. But if it is not a master, the entity will generally fade away into oblivion.

The Master takes you out of the body. It is left as though a suit of clothes and you are shown the wonders of the universe. There are other ways of getting out of the body but this way is the soundest, and the one in which you are certain of no harm. The way of the sacred mushroom in Mexico, used by certain cults, is under the guidance of a priest. But there is peyote, and mescaline, and a number of other drugs which can take one out of his body. The latter are usually done at the expense of the individual and you can never tell what is going to happen if you are not trained in leaving the body, and allowing it to stay intact until the return of the spirit. If the body should pass away, or be buried by mistake, then the spirit may not be able to find another one or adjust outside of it for considerable time and thus he becomes a wandering entity which might bring harm to those in the physical body.

Many are able to leave their body, but do so unknowingly. Some do it during sleep, and yet it is recorded and remembered during their awakening hours. Peter spoke of his Self as the glorious body, and throughout the Bible there were references of the Self as being used by those who know how. There is the reference of Jesus when about to be seized by those in a mob, and he disappeared from their sight. There is another reference of him on the mount, and there appeared to him a couple of prophets and he became transfigured. There is the story of his rising from the tomb and appearing to the apostles in the upper chamber. Now Christianity makes something great out of the ability which Jesus used his other body, and seem to think that nobody other than he could do this. However, his apostles had the same ability, and many in ancient times in the land of Judea could make their appearances in two places at the same time. Yet he told an audience, according to St. John's scripture, that any man could do what he could and better!

One of the first things a master teaches his disciples is the ability to get out of his body at will. This was the first thing I showed you— but this isn't a subtle reference that I'm a master. My knowledge of those things which a master teaches his disciple are great, that is because I have always wanted to learn and took time and effort to do so. Since anyone who has knowledge cannot store it no more than a man can take money out of circulation, he must impart this knowledge openly to someone else or a wide group. I therefore must give you what knowledge that I know and to others through my writings. To give knowledge without discrimination is, in the words of Jesus, "to cast the pearls before the swine." In other words one must be careful to whom he gives his knowledge and what he gives them, otherwise two things can happen to him: First, the very knowledge of life which he gives out to a person can be used on him, by the receiver, and secondly, the receiver of the knowledge can take it lightly and throw it away. Thereby the giver has wasted his time and his effort upon someone who was not of mental, moral and spiritual strength to receive the message. So you must be careful of what you tell anyone about the occult teachings.

One of the earliest groups who used the out-of-body-experiences, were the Magi. The Magi were a group of magicians who studied the spiritual problems of their day sometime along about 500 B.C. to maybe 500 A.D., and there are some remnants of this cult still existing today. They were descendants of Zoroastraianism, and of a very high order. It was said that the three wise men who visited Christ at the time of his birth, were Magi members sent by their master in Persia to greet the savior as he came into the world. They knew by signs and prophecies that a world teacher was coming, and where he would exactly be born, and the conditions of his life. He was found by a Magi, out of his body, and reported to the Magi master, who sent the three Magi to greet Christ with their gifts. The other part of the legend goes like this— they went in their spiritual bodies, manifesting at the gates of the city riding camels, so that their physical bodies could be seen by those incapable of having second sight and their visit recorded.

I have pointed out that this out-of-the-body-experience is most important, and that the 7th spiritual problem is leaving the body daily, and seeing that it dies and is renewed when spirit returns. St. Paul's letters have constant references to this: "the man who was caught up in heaven three days, etc." The Acts of the Apostles also makes many references. This is the keystone of the spiritual life. Learn it!

More later.

Letters to Gail

July 5, 1963

Dear Gail:

The eighth topic for discussion is "How Does Idealism Affect The Drive of The Spirit?" By the word drive I mean activity and goal of the Jivatma. Often the word spirit denotes the Jivatma, and other times it denotes the special fluid of life which penetrates all things giving it the living spark of life.

Idealism is any theory which affirms the central importance of mind, or the spiritual and ideal, in reality. Example of this might be – the individual has his values in beauty, in God, or in those general values of honesty, love, kindness, etc. There isn't much difference in values and idealism. Values make up the ideal, and qualities of God make for the whole – like mercy, kindness, love, etc.

Idealism is sort of a fast, like a physical fast, when one begins to live by it. He no longer is interested in certain things like the mass man who lives by his automobile, radio, family habits, job and other things which keep him from enjoying the spiritual fruits. This is the way we must keep the spirit up provided we are not in the higher level with the masters. It is only the spiritual qualities for which we are striving anyway and the fight against entrapment by the negative forces are not of any reasoning for the drive of the Jivatma. When one attempts to take up the spiritual path his constant striving to reach that goal which is commonly known as the Unity with God, (although this is called the Unity with God it is not that at all) he must link himself with that unreasonable ambition and fiery desire to finally get his goal or perish in the attempt. This terrible struggle of the Jivatma of the individual is often seen in the Christian mystics whose hardships are displayed by the church. So very true, for their struggle against the enslavement of the negative forces is awful, and I have no other example to give you than that of many of the Christian saints, e.g., St. Augustine who had to give up his mistress and all the luxuries of life in order to enter into the spiritual life. St. Francis went through the terrible hardships to reach his goal.

Is there any other way of getting there? The only way that I know is through the masters, and often the path is hard because of the karma of the individual. But when the church shifts its grounds as much as it does today to meet the political and economical problems of modern times, one soon forgets the real goal of life. Therefore the drive of the Jivatma depends upon the desires it has for reaching its goal with God. This desire is usually based upon the idealism placed before it by the Masters, and if the idealism is any different from that of the highest order, the Jivatma will keep failing until put back upon the right path again. This idealism must consist of at least three things: 1. Worship of God; 2. Adoration of God; 3. Reverence of God. There is a difference in the three. The worship of God consists in singing praises, etc. The Adoration of God is to see his handiwork in all things, be it in the negative world, or the worlds of the positive, and the reverence of God is that in which you will revere Him as the total – all entities being of his handicraft, and all things belonging to him. Prayer enters into the latter part.

Desire is the basic wish for entering into the highest Kingdom. This may be a paradox for you, but understand this that where I have preached non-attachment to anything also applies to a non-attachment to God. One of the followers of Buddha, and I believe that his name was Tao Sheng, a Chinese philosopher, about 400 A.D. had this to say about the subject: "If you want the truth to stand clear before you, never be for or against it. The struggle between "for" and "against" is the mind's worse disease; while the deep meaning is misunderstood, it is useless to meditate on Rest, etc." Later in his writings he says this "The more you talk about It (The Absolute), the more you think about It, the further from It you go; stop talking, stop thinking, and there is nothing you will not understand. Return to the Root and you will find its meaning; pursue the Light, and you will lose its source: Look inward, and in a flash you will conquer the Apparent and the Void. For the whirligigs of Apparent and Void all come from mistaken views. There is no need to seek Truth; only stop having views. Do not accept either position, examine it or pursue it; at the least thought of "Is" and "Isn't," there is chaos and the Mind is lost. Though the two exist because of the One, do not cling to the One; only when no thought arises are the Dharmas without blame."

All Tao Sheng is saying is that you can have the drive of the idealism as long as you are dwelling in the mind area, but once you step into the spiritual path you are now ready to drop all that went on before, and begin to live in that world which is of the spirit, or the true world of God. Here in this world is the happiness which man or the spirit of man is seeking— and he is looking for that which is perfect no longer, for here is perfection, but he must always be seeking a mite more perfection, as the Zen Buddhist is, for that perfection is always short of fulfillment. This is as Tao Sheng says: "Being is an aspect of Non-Being; Non-being is an aspect of Being. The One is none other than the All, the All none other than the One. Take your stand on this, and the rest will follow of its own accord."

Now what I'm saying is this. One meets with this problem of idealism which affects the drive of the spirit towards its goal, but quickly as he learns that it isn't important then it is dropped and he progresses faster. But he will have the problem because he thinks that it is important to starve for God, to struggle to get into the realms of heaven and to suffer the hardships which are apparent if he wants to take that route. This is the route that all Christian saints have taken. For example, St. Teresa used to gather up her nuns, in her nunnery, and shout to them "Let's storm the gates of heaven! Let us take it by force!" This is a reversal of the true way of getting into the heavenly world, and it appears to me that if she or any other western saint tried such tactics they were not very far advanced on the spiritual path. This is part of the aggressive habit which the westerners built in themselves which is supposedly for success, material or spiritual.

So again, I say that once you have bypassed this problem you will be further along the path toward the real goal. You won't have to undergo many of the hardships which so many of the neophytes do when they are striving to get through problems which are not even apparent to them. It is a hardship for anyone to recognize his own problems much less those which are spiritual and hidden within himself. We are always able to see the problems of others much better than our own, but it is really not their problem which we are seeing but our own which is reflecting from the mirror which we have placed in them.

I don't expect any of these letters to solve any problems for you, but they may help you see and know what they might be and that is always a start. If you are to ask anyone about any problem you might have, it would be a mistake, except if you approached a Master, and I doubt if he would ever say anything.

More later.

July 7, 1963

Dear Gail:

This is problem nine, "The Nature of the Spiritual Energies," which I presume is one of the higher studies of the spiritual science. It is one which I've had a lot of study from Master Singh and has been the basis for the Audible Life Stream. The spiritual energies are only those energy streams which come out of each plane, originally from the highest source where is supposedly the Throne of The Absolute! You have had some parts of this scattered through the letters and in both THE TIGER'S FANG, and THE FLUTE OF GOD. Also in other writings of mine you have seen references made to the spiritual energies!

The Audible Life Stream is that upon which all life is dependent. It leaves the highest heaven like a radio beam, in a wide circle, going out in waves; but as it leaves that plane for its downward descent, it flows into the channel which will send the energy out over that particular plane like a radio beam. The channel is always the deity of that particular plane, and through him flows the spiritual energy to be distributed to that region, and it will flow likewise through the lesser deities on the same plane in a likewise manner. Thus it goes downward in the same pattern until it reaches the lowest plane where it has now become a negative power instead of a positive power. This spiritual power becomes a negative force after reaching the third lower plane, and I suspect that it is this way because it cannot reach that far below and still stay in the positive force. Again, I suspect likewise that it might be that the Absolute has willed it this way in order to establish the barrier for the Jivatma to make its way upward and through the lower regions. If the Jivatma has any power to make its movement upward toward the God region, it makes use of the negative force to make this step.

As the Audible Life Stream descends into the planes below, each plane has a distinctive sound. One first hears the sound of the cricket, then the flute, the bells, roaring of waterfalls, birds chirping, violin, and the drums. These are distinctive on each plane, and each plane's subdivisions will likewise have a sound which one will come to hear, when the senses become subtle enough. It is the whirling of the atoms out of the heavens above which make these sounds, as they pass through each plane going into the next below. These sounds are wondrous sounds and can be heard even at times when one is not in contemplation. The reason that many masters seek the heights of mountains to meditate, is that the silence which goes with the higher regions, and the rarified atmosphere, will give one an opportunity to hear these sounds. So many spiritual seekers have found their goals in the mountain—the biographies of the spiritual persons, saints and masters show that most of them have chosen the mountains for meditation.

These spiritual energies are those which the individual lives upon. Jesus said, "Man does not live by bread alone!" This was his statement to the people who were ignorant, for should he tell them of the spiritual energies they might have had two reactions; first, many might have wanted to give up their lives and follow him, and secondly, he might have had a rebellious group on hand. None may have believed him! But the spiritual energies are in the body— and are divided into five parts. Adana, Udana, and the others I have forgotten, but they pertain to individual parts of the body where each one resides. The Udana energy is in the stomach area, and the Adana is in the chest and heart area. Other areas are: limbs, lower and upper, thighs and sex organs, and finally the head area.

I've done for you two letters already on the Audible Life Current, so there won't be much need for taking up this again, however, as I pointed out in THE TIGER'S FANG as one approaches the great astral city, Sahasra-Dal-Kanwal, the great lights flashing out of the top of what apparently seems like a crater; and these lights are colored streams. In reality these lights are various streams of spiritual energies, which I'm now speaking of. They flow out of the astral city, throughout the astral world into the physical world, and become the suns and moons of the worlds of this universe. This world of the suns and moons, and of course stars, is one across which the traveler must cross in order to enter into the first region of the spiritual universes.

In the book History and Power of the Mind, *by Ingelese, (in the Public Library) detail study is given to these powers on this plane. Even in this world the energies still make their play as powers, with many colors as a reflection of these power streams flowing out of the great astral city. Every day science is coming forward with a new discovery about the spiritual energies in this world, as if they had found something startling and new for the peoples of the earth. However, most occultists or spiritual students know, or have known the sources and workings of the spiritual energies for years; science is only centuries behind.*

The greater the refinement of any individual, the closer he is to the primal source of the Audible Life Current. This force penetrates all—from the rosebud to the star, and it is the sound or music which all religious groups sing their praises. It is generally known to the world as the heavenly music – and so many times one might tune in on it without knowing of its existence only to report of having heard that wonderful, divine music. It is said that Johann Sebastian Bach heard these beautiful sounds and recorded it in his music for the world; also Beethoven was supposed to have recorded his music from the Audible Life Current. In either case I can say for certain that their music is the most classical of all earthly music. It is supposedly said that all elements of music are contained in Bach's compositions, that he wrote the perfect score of music.

The nature of these spiritual energies will be confronted when one first steps out on the path and the seeker will be asking his master about them. He will seek out the answers regardless of who has his destiny in hand, but often will receive no answer from his Guru, because it may not be the proper time for his instruction in the spiritual energies. But the spiritual energies have only one purpose, rather have a singular nature – that is for the growth of the consciousness of all things, be it in the rock and mineral, stone, or in the highest apex of life – that of the human being! This consciousness will serve its purpose to put that entity which is enclosed inside it, be it a rock or homo sapiens, into the mind to make its effort toward its true home again. We cannot overlook this fact and when one tries to make a great fact out of the nature of life – which is actually the nature of the spiritual energies – he is only making a complex subject out of a simple one! You cannot get beyond the fact that the spiritual energies are for the only purpose—that is growth. Even the reincarnation of the individual is for growth and it is using the spiritual energies for its promotion of growth. The consciousness in a rock must grow until it becomes something else, and so upward in the chain of evolution goes the growth of the individual consciousness until it reaches the Jivatma stage and then starts its journey to God again.

More later.

Letters to Gail

July 8, 1963

Dear Gail:

This is the tenth problem, "How Does Priori Knowledge Exist As Spiritual Knowledge?"

Priori knowledge means religious knowledge, as that of houses of certain religious orders as the Dominican or Augustinian, etc. The religious knowledge which exists in those orders are not the same as the layman gets from the outside ministering. All religious groups, Buddhism, Christianity, Mohammed, Sufism, and others have houses of religious orders who have been advanced quite spiritually. However, those houses of religious orders are generally not connected with any outside activity at all. Take, for example, the Trappist monks who live in silence and have so very little contact with the outer world if any!

The knowledge which these groups have, I speak now of the Trappists, is or must certainly be much greater than the ones which have an outer contact. Take, for example, the writings of Thomas Merton, a Trappist, who has been very productive for the past few years, since his first book, The Seven-Story Mountain! *These show the result of a contact with the very high planes— these writings are extremely lofty! St. Augustine wrote a very lofty book when he did the* City of God! *There are other books, but you will notice that most of the knowledge is not quite at the top level where we would think in terms of Spiritual knowledge— most of it is still in the mental realm chewing over the various points in diatribes on Spiritual matters. I have a book in my collection called the* Sar Bachan *written by Sardar Seva Singh, which is the teachings of the Sound Current, and acts as practically my Bible!*

This book is a volume of priori knowledge because as all books do, including all the sacred scriptures, must approach the spiritual with and through the psychic senses. This is the exact definition of the apriori knowledge— that which approaches the Absolute through the inner senses, or through the inner doors! This is exactly what many of those inner religious orders do—i.e., the Sufi order, and other mystical groups, and are always doing. The inner senses, or those ten inner doors, always leads the seeker into priori knowledge – they are the gateways for the knowledge to enter into the area of the Jivatma, or for the Jivatma to leave the shell or what may be called the body to reach the knowledge regions. It is a concern that one realize these gateways so that he might recognize at times what or where comes that knowledge of life!

There is little knowledge in the negative world unless it is knowledge which is for the benefit of the body. It is that work of Kal (negative) power which traps the Jivatma and keeps it intact in the physical regions. You see the Kal Power, or the Kal Niranjan, the ruler of the region and his sub-chiefs are to take the Jivatma in hand, at birth in this universe, as though it were the teacher– and many times it will substitute itself like a Guru, and so many times you may think that the Kal Niranjan is the Guru and follow him. He leads you along a narrow path filled with pleasures of the negative sort, and from this path the Jivatma may be pushed into the depths of hell. But then one can recognize the pathway of the beautiful side of life, the real knowledge which is there, and the Guru who is always waiting patiently for the neophtye to turn to him and lead him into the far realms of heaven. This comes through the realization that the Audible Life Current is always trying to speak to the individual.

Anyone who can quote scriptures, or the words of Shakespeare, or great men of this earth, is called great and is praised. But such praise is not substantial. It is just like the braying of an ass which starts in very loud and gradually gets weaker. Knowledge of this nature is never enduring. Only that knowledge is real which is uniform from the beginning to the end, or it may grow stronger with time. This is the way of that knowledge which is gained from the time spent in listening to the Audible Life Current. The yoga called Raja Yoga is always one of the pathways in which one can travel to gain this esoteric knowledge.

This esoteric knowledge, which is another name for priori knowledge, is that which one must gain before becoming proficient in the art of spirituality. Esoteric means that which is designed for, and understood by, the specially initiated alone, or that which belongs to the circle initiated in such teachings. Private knowledge of the higher realms. This private knowledge is concerned with the five melodies which man hears and which corresponds with the five great melodies of the universe. Remember my letter in which I spoke of the Hindi names for the melodies.

The Upanishads in the Hindi sacred scriptures means that the knowledge of which I am speaking is stored together within these writings. There is another place where such wisdom is also stored in writings, and that is in the Proverbs of the old Bible. Buddha gives the esoteric knowledge in what is called "The Three Baskets" and the same is in the Zen Buddhist precepts, the Sar Bachan, Kabir's poetry and the writings of Rumi, the Persian poet. These are a few who have given the esoteric knowledge in words, and a very difficult task also. I forgot one of the greatest of writings in this line comes from the pen of Hazrat Inayat Khan who was one of the great violinists of modern times. He died in the latter part of 1930's. Most of the Sufis, (Khan was one) have something important to say on the esoteric knowledge.

The knowledge of the divine goes like this: 1. Esoteric, the highest; 2. priori, the middle knowledge, and 3. the worldly or outside knowledge, like that we gain in school, or from life's experience. The esoteric knowledge comes from practicing meditation in which you listen to the Audible Life Current. The priori knowledge can come from the same way, only on lower planes, and the worldly knowledge comes from that which we get from books, and experience in this life outside. Once you catch the division of the three, it won't be hard to find one's self going in to comtemplate so you can make use of any of the three. It isn't easy, but there is little need of worrying about any of the methods for there isn't any problem at hand by which the Jivatma will have too much difficulty in solving to reach them once it has taken up the goal to reach the Absolute.

Then the paradox comes about like this: the esoteric knowledge and the priori knowledge can become one provided that the ends are similar in their appraoch. I am saying this, that if the group in a religious order, or two or more are seeking the answer to something, they may get it through priori knowledge – from books, meditation or out-of-body experience. Except for books, the same knowledge may be gained as esoteric but it's when that knowledge comes down from the higher planes instead of the Jivatma going up to receive. Often it does this and on the lower planes mixes with the priori knowledge and becomes that, and thereby gives you the answer to this question – because "it, priori knowledge, exists as spiritual knowledge under such a circumstance."

More later.

July 10, 1963

Dear Gail:

The subject is "The Limitations of Knowledge, " which is the eleventh spiritual problem. This appears to be a paradox of what I have been telling you previously, and what you read or hear what so many others who have studied Occultism have to say!

Therefore all knowledge regardless of whether it might be the God knowledge or the earth knowledge has limitations upon itself. This hardly seems possible when we are constantly storing away knowledge, of facts and figures, in our minds. The realm of knowledge seems unlimited in its wide, vast depths of data on this plane alone, but even so it has a limitation because all it is doing is a repeat of the original, and alter-ising the appearance of what it might be. The changing, or adding to the piece of original data is called alter-ising, as you remember in the letter on the Four Conditions of Life!

This situation on knowledge is upward through the Astral world, and the Brahm world to the border of the country of Sat Desh. It is there where the mind is dropped and Soul enters into the beginning of the true spiritual world as pure Jivatma! Here it is the spiritual knowledge which counts, and there again is a vast realm of truth which the Jivatma must absorb in order to prepare itself for the final entrance into the highest kingdom of God. Since the data in these realms are of the pure nature the Jivatma is given a very slow pace by the Master so he will not become over logged – or have spiritual indigestion. This is a condition which is extremely true of the Jivatma in this area trying to absorb these truths. In a manner of speaking these truths are so strong that often a Jivatma becomes too ill– I'm using the word ill for the lack of a better word– and cannot continue on his upward journey. Often the Master will return him to earth and there await until this period of spiritual sickness is over before attempting the journey again.

This state may occur at any point in the Sat Desh worlds, for the greatest condition which the Jivatma must face is that of confronting Sat Nam, the ruler of the Fifth plane, which is in this world. Sat Nam is actually a reflection of the individual Jivatma, for upon viewing the Ruler of this plane, the Jivatma will exclaim to himself, "That is I;

I am that!" However, if the Jivatma cannot (rather has any aberrations left within itself), it cannot face the great Sat Nam, the first representative of God in the lower plane of Sat Desh! This is when the Jivatma falls into a spiritual sickness and must return again to the worlds below in order to see what is the cause of his condition, rest and return later!

Here is the paradoxical condition of knowledge— only the spiritual knowledge is accepted by the Jivatma, regardless of how impure it might be in reaching itself. When on the lower planes the mind accepts the worldly knowledge, but once it has reached the borders of the Sat Desh worlds, the mind is dropped as the last vestige of the lower bodies and the Jivatma travels as the nude self. Here upon, the Jivatma makes the journey accepting the truth as itself— the mind cannot accept the truth, it can only reflect truth, while the Jivatma can accept truth. This is one of the great paradoxical subjects which one can study in the occult sciences. Nobody seems to know too much about this except the masters, and they seldom will make a direct reference; but always carry it as an indirectness which one must learn for himself.

Now the limitations of knowledge lies in the fact that knowledge ends when one reaches the second plane of the Sat Desh world, called the Agam Purusha plane— and thereafter enters into the full plane of intuition or the world of sensitivity— this is a world of feeling in which the knowledge, if you wish to call it knowledge, can enter into the Jivatma in a sense of absorption instead of direct presentation as in the case of the lower planes. This is a viewpoint which must be established in your thoughts before you can actually get an overall view of the worlds of knowledge.

These worlds of knowledge are many; they are vast, but there is a limitation to them. The feeling which one must develop upon passing through these worlds of knowledge is that of a goodwill, not love, but a compassion of the feelings instead of the intellectual. The Christians preach love, Buddhists preach something akin to love, and most of the orthodox persons go into a dido over the word love, and acclaim it as the highest quality of the individual, and make noises over something which they call the love of God for man! Frankly, I don't know what they are talking about. But this feeling is a neutral feeling, not a compassion as Buddha spoke of, but a sort of goodwill, which makes you open to understanding, wisdom and spiritual relationships!

Knowledge alone doesn't carry one past the barriers, but it must become a two-fold path, of knowledge and goodwill, which in the end gains the means as one wishes. You must however put the right kind of knowledge into the mind so that it will reflect outwardly— this is the rule of the road in other worlds— for you cannot let the mind go astray, as I pointed out in the letter on depth psychology. This type of study however is so far in advance on depth psychology that it is doubltful whether the psychologists actually know what I'm talking about, and if so, how much would they accept it. This is because none have had any experience in this world—and they are not prepared to believe anything that is said or done in the matter of the higher spiritual studies. You must remember that in dealing with the laws of the negative world— or what are known as the laws of nature, the psychologists are not apt to get themselves involved in anything further.

You see these people are playing a big game of sharpening the intellect. They do not wish to evolve into a higher state of learning or spirituality, because they as a whole have little use of the religious side of man—they think of it as the aberration, and in a sense they are right, but mostly wrong because the limitations of learning is there. What they learn beyond the fundamentals of psychology seems to be nothing, except a repeat as I said before! When they run out of games to play, more are invented to keep the game going. This is true of the postal department of the U.S., if you will notice— a sprawling organization which has completed its usefulness and is now in the decline, is an example of a group trying to play games.

As you will notice that one must enter into heaven, if that is what the highest world is called, in the state of feeling, and with whatever knowledge which has been passed on by the Master, and that absorbed into the self through the spiritual senses of the Jivatma. Together, these two qualities will carry the Jivatma into the lap of the Absolute!

Nothing can tell you the exact limits of knowledge in any of the worlds, but you must be prepared to understand that there are limitations and one must be able to compare them with the knowledge he learns on other planes. This alone will give him the limitations of knowledge as the absolving of the problems along the spiritual path.

More later.

July 12, 1963

Dear Gail:

The twelfth spiritual problem is: "The Limitations of the Spiritual Force (the positive) in the lower Worlds," and is the subject of this letter and the last of the problems for discussion. There are dozens of other problems or questions which the neophyte must face in his journey into the higher worlds but this is the coverage of the major ones, and most of the others will be taken off these I have been discussing up to now.

The positive spiritual force works on the higher planes, above the Brahm world, and is the force which gives power to all worlds, but it is limited to working in the upper worlds, because of the refinement of its nature. In a way I don't know how to put it but the positive or Purusha power, which Master Singh always called the Master Power will not enter into this world below – its fineness of character will not allow it to operate in this universe despite Dr. Norman Vincent Peale's theory called the "Power of Positive Thinking!" This is why the negative power is in force– and the counteracting of the two makes up the lower worlds. In this lower world the Law works accordingly– and it works through people and through plants, animal life, etc. The Law will make any individual pay who doesn't live up to its demands– and this is because being the Law of Karma it cannot let anyone escape! Only those who are under the care of the Master will escape the law and can live outside it! Nobody appears to know that the law is entrapping them so they cannot get into the spiritual land. Now those who break the law are actually trying to get out of it, when those who are obeying it so steadfast and so praise the law and yell to respect the law are those whom the law has actually entrapped! They believe in the moral philosophy of the churches and the respectability of mankind! This is a poor philosophy, but I don't go around preaching this to anyone openingly because they would think that I'm needed for the bughouse!

The positive force can come into the lower worlds, but it must come through a Guru, the only way, and be distributed to his own disciples and to those with whom he contacts. The Guru is a pole for the power, in the lower world, and the one whom God has chosen to act as his intermediary hero. He has the power and ability to place it where he wishes and that person whom he powers out his love upon is the lucky one who will receive most of the power. You can only think in the limited terms of looking at a body which a Master wears and wonder if it be true that this person is capable of the great things told about him. Look at Gandhi for instance– weak, little man without any apparent physical strength, had nothing but a loin cloth, pair of glasses, and a cheap watch. Yet a man of great spiritual strength because he allowed himself to be opened as a channel through God.

Every thousand years a great spiritual teacher comes to this earth to revitalize it! He pours out a powerful ray of positive spiritual force which carries through to all living things and once again the power is predominate over all things! Life blooms, a strong religious trend springs up again, but it goes through a cycle and once again dies away, but is caught up at the end of its cycle by another spiritual messenger who carries the force again to this world. The power is there and all things are made new again! I don't know who is the present true master here now, nor do I know who was the past.

So-called spiritual practices, as we know them in churches, the rites and rituals which are symbols supposedly for the release of energies, only open the channels for the negative forces – not evil mind you – but the negative creative power which doesn't have the power of the positive forces. You can create or bring yourself into the position of being the recipient of that desire wished by bringing this negative power into your life. Do you understand? This is what I'm trying to say– "The Power of Positive Thinking," as advanced by Dr. Peale is doing just this thing, as I've spoken of. The negative forces work in the field of the materialistic–money, living with the better aids of life, insurance, sex, homes, and well, just about anything you can name in daily living, clothing, etc. Of course one can receive these things by working with the negative forces – and this is well explained in the History and Power of Mind *by Ingalese, if you care to read it. It's in the public library!*

The problem of receiving the positive or Purusha power from the higher planes remains one of these which must be solved by going into the realms above the negative worlds. Once the Jivatma hears the life Sound Current, which is part of the positive current, he has had a touch of God and he doesn't want to live the life which you can find around you in this civilization. He wants only to get into that life above these lower worlds and dwell in the bliss which is there. He must go upward— he feels the urge to get into those realms where he can have nothing but the greatness of the Absolute!

There is a difference in the positive powers and the negative powers, mainly that the latter is made up of a forming power, as I have explained in THE FLUTE OF GOD! That power which is above the worlds of the negative is both the forming power and the healing power. It is a power which brings to the Jivatma wisdom, bliss and love. The lower power brings the opposite qualities into one's life! Therefore when the entrapment of the negative forces comes around you, then one must turn his attention to the opposite qualities, not those miseries which come with the trap of this universe. The church teaches us that we must suffer in this life as Christ did— this is a statement which is certainly a negative one— and that which entraps the person all over again! They simply don't understand what their own savior was incapable of doing— Jesus couldn't overcome mob violence against truth! This was the law of the negative power working, against him, through the mob! As I spoke of before, if he had dispelled the law to work in his own favor then he would have upset the balance of the lower worlds and would have gone against the Will of God! The only way for him to have sidestepped his crucifixion would have been to put himself up to the higher planes, which he was apparently able to do as shown later when he ascended into heaven in full physical form.

A theory which I've toyed with for a long time is that perhaps he wasn't in the body which was hung on the cross. Perhaps he mocked up a body to look like his own and left it for the Roman soldiers to nail to the cross, and the mob to mock. He could have even been in the crowd which witnessed the scene of his supposed death on the cross! This is sacrilegious according to the church, but it is a theory which I've long mulled over. Of course he had already left the body when it was nailed there, but many never think of it in terms of this.

You can reach out and grasp this positive spiritual power on your own, it isn't hard, nor does it need a master all the time. You must look to the higher powers, at least all times in your life.

More later.

Paul

July 14, 1963

Dear Gail:

This is the final letter on this series, but don't be discouraged for there is another idea buzzing around in my head to do as a project for you. It will come into manifestation shortly!

It would be good to summarize the full contents of what I've written previously but it seems that you already know the letters well enough to let this thought drop. Instead I will use the space for the discussion of the Razor-Edged Path, as it is called. First, I will give you an old Swiss parable: It seems that before Switzerland became a Christian nation one of the old Irish priests who was sent there as a missionary to convert the people gave a sermon at the beginning of his mission that martyrs were their best intercessors before God. The good peasants of alpine Switzerland being simple and realistic people believed him and took his word so completely that they killed him. And what happened was that it worked: they became Christians! The point I'm trying to make is: The path to God is certainly a Razor-Edged Path, and when treading it one must live boldly and dangerously. It is only the bold who will reach the heights of heaven!

Any reason for turning to the Absolute is sufficient. An old Sadhu who believed he was ready to leave this earth decided to teach a few pupils the knowledge he had gained during his life. Each applicant for his group had an excuse for wanting to gain the knowledge– one said his wife was merciless to him; another claimed he saw miracles in all living things; one claimed humility, etc. At the end of the interview the old Sadhu accepted all the applicants for his group saying that any reason for turning to God was sufficient. This reminds me that once I approached a Holy Man and asked him if he could show me the way to use the power to gain some money, but he replied, "I know nothing about money, but I can show you the way to use the power to gain God!" Completely reversed my thinking at that moment and set my feet back on the path again!

You don't have to believe in God at the beginning of the study of the Spiritual Path. All one has to do is to practice the spiritual discipline and eventually he will not only come to believe in God but he will also experience the great reality. Belief about God and knowing God are two different things. Belief is subject to limited and misleading information and doubt, but knowing from personal experience is not. The spiritual master says that a newcomer to the religious life is not expected to know what is knowable only through direct God-Realization. There are timeless methods of testing and developing one's vast innate potentialities. The disciplines include contemplation—the mastery of emotions and mind; study—familiarization with one's own constitution and the laws of spiritual life; and service – how to exact the most productive results from every expenditure of thought and energy.

By following these disciplines, the teachers promise, you will soon discover that your most extraordinary inherent capacities are of a spiritual nature, and that true greatness of being is potentially within you. And as you learn to utilize these newfound capacities, they say, you will attain those new states of consciousness in which you will directly experience, in fullest awareness and beyond all possible doubt, the ability of incommunicable knowledge of God.

The path has an end although it never seems to be one. You must go back to the letter on Beingness in order to see what I've just said, for it is actually being that which you are!

The second part of the aspects of spiritual aspiration is: the need to recognize rather than to acquire. To anyone who feels his inadequacy the Master will say: "You are like the man who is sitting on a bag of diamonds bemoaning his poverty. You are like the man who possesses a ship and worries over the weather. You are like the man who owns a library and hasn't time to read. You are like the man who is the inheritor of the greatest kingdom yet lives the life of a beggar. The diamonds represent your physical potentiality; the ship and sea represents your emotional potentiality; the library represents your mental potentality and the kingdom represents your spiritual potentiality. Therefore you possess all you need. There is nothing to acquire. You have only to learn to recognize what is already yours."

Most of those who come into the religious life do so for a selfish purpose; they want something: food, shelter, money, power, pleasant work, no illness, greater talent. Jesus' words, "What things soever ye desire when ye pray, believe that ye receive them and ye shall have them." But the true motive for treading the razor's edged path is because one wishes to do so, mostly for joy and peace which are unknown outside the spiritual way. Generally it is because of love to know God and to do His will that causes one to take up this path. The subtlest danger in spiritual learning is to substitute faith in book knowledge, or blind faith in authority, for direct experience. This is so in both East and West where many religiously minded people confuse an emotional-devotional attachment or an intellectual attitude with an experiential belief in a sacred scripture.

I must be absolutely honest about what I know and what I do not know in spiritual knowledge. I must always have discrimination enough to recognize what I unmistakeably know, and integrity enough to question what I only surmise may be true. I am constantly faced with the facts of my own experience, while on the other hand, the hypotheses suggested to me by others. One of the grave dangers of organized religion lies in the tendency to ask the devotee to simply accept a creed or dogma rather than to insist that he investigate it diligently in his own life through contemplation, study and service.

Nothing then is to be accepted upon authority— for there are many authorities making claims for God and many gods. I do not accept anything on reason because spiritual truth is intuitively perceived in a realm which transcends the limitations of the everyday mind. It is essentially a matter of individual investigation; for contemplating and testing in one's own life; and for affirming through direct realization of its truth in higher consciousness. The difference between the aspirant after truth and the disciple of the Master is that the former is able to say that "I believe," and the disciple says, "I know!"

The true knowledge of God is obtainable in two ways: through the revelation of God in holy scriptures and the testimonies of saints, and through one's own immediate intuitive experience of reality. The knowledge of God professed by most religious people is based on accepting scriptural teachings as revelation. The knowledge transmitted by the saints of all religions is derived from personal experiences of God-Realization. This personal experience of God comes from beyond normal reasoning!

This is the final letter of this series. I will start another set of readership material shortly. Be patient with me.

Finis.

Paul

ECKANKAR Presents a Spiritual Study Course: *Soul Travel—The Illuminated Way*

People want to know the secrets of life and death. In response to this need Paul Twitchell, the modern-day founder of Eckankar, brought to light the Spiritual Exercises of ECK—which offer a direct way to God.

Those who are ready to begin a study of Eckankar can receive special monthly discourses which give clear, simple instructions for these exercises. The first twelve-month series is called *Soul Travel—The Illuminated Way*. Mailed each month, the discourses are designed to lead the individual to the Light and Sound of God.

The techniques in these discourses, when practiced twenty minutes a day, are likely to prove survival beyond death. Many have used them as a direct route to Self-Realization, where one learns his mission in life. The next stage, God Consciousness, is the joyful state wherein Soul becomes the spiritual traveler, an agent for God. The underlying principle one learns then is this: "Soul exists because God loves It."

Discourses include these titles, among others: "The Universality of Soul Travel," "The Illuminated Way by Direct Projection," and "The Spiritual Cities of This World." These can be studied at home or with fellow students in a local Eckankar class—look in the phone book under Eckankar, or write us for classes in your area.

For more information on how to receive *Soul Travel—The Illuminated Way* and Eckankar classes in your area, use the coupon at the back of this book, or write:

ECKANKAR
P.O. Box 27300
Minneapolis, MN 55427 U.S.A.

Introductory Books on ECKANKAR
The Ancient Science of Soul Travel

The Wind of Change, Sri Harold Klemp

What are the hidden spiritual reasons behind every event in your life? With stories drawn from his own life-long training, Eckankar's spiritual leader shows you how to use the power of Spirit to discover those reasons. Follow him from the Wisconsin farm of his youth, to a military base in Japan; from a job in Texas, into the realms beyond, as he shares the secrets of Eckankar.

In My Soul I Am Free, Brad Steiger

Here is the incredible life story of Paul Twitchell—prophet, healer, Soul Traveler—whose spiritual exercises have helped thousands to contact the Light and Sound of God. Brad Steiger lets the famed ECK Master tell you in his own words about Soul Travel, healing in the Soul body, the role of dreams and sleep, and more. Includes a spiritual exercise called "The Easy Way."

ECKANKAR—The Key to Secret Worlds, Paul Twitchell

Paul Twitchell, modern-day founder of Eckankar, gives you the basics of this ancient teaching. Includes six specific Soul Travel exercises to see the Light and hear the Sound of God, plus case histories of Soul Travel. Learn to recognize yourself as Soul—and journey into the heavens of the Far Country.

The Tiger's Fang, Paul Twitchell

Paul Twitchell's teacher, Rebazar Tarzs, takes him on a journey through vast worlds of Light and Sound, to sit at the feet of the spiritual Masters. Their conversations bring out the secret of how to draw closer to God—and awaken Soul to Its spiritual destiny. Many have used this book, with its vivid descriptions of heavenly worlds and citizens, to begin their own spiritual adventures.

For more free information about the books and teachings of Eckankar, please write:

ECKANKAR, P.O. Box 27300, Minneapolis, MN 55427 U.S.A.

Or look under ECKANKAR in your local phone book for an Eckankar center near you.

For Free Information on ECKANKAR...

☐ Yes, I want free information on Eckankar. Please send me brochures on the Eckankar books and on the twelve-month study series, *Soul Travel—The Illuminated Way*.

☐ I would like information on the nearest Eckankar discussion or study group in my area.

Please type or print clearly 941

Name____

Street____

City________________________**State/Prov.**__________

Zip/Postal Code__________**Country**__________________

(Our policy: Your name and address are held in strict confidence—we do not rent or sell our mailing lists. Nor will we send anyone to call on you.)

ECKANKAR
P.O. Box 27300
Minneapolis, MN 55427
U.S.A.